NOSH
QUICK & EASY
& the family team by Joy May

NOSH SUGAR-FREE GLUTEN-FREE
SAYING 'NO' TO PROCESSED SUGAR AND GLUTEN NEVER TASTED SO GOOD

JOY MAY

ISBN: 9780993260919

NOSH GLUTEN-FREE BAKING
ANOTHER NO-FUSS, GLUTEN-FREE COOKBOOK FROM THE MAY FAMILY

JOY MAY

ISBN: 9780956746498

NOSH GLUTEN-FREE
A NO-FUSS, EVERYDAY GLUTEN-FREE COOKBOOK FROM THE MAY FAMILY

JOY MAY

ISBN: 9780956746450

NOSH QUICK & EASY
ANOTHER NO-NONSENSE SIMPLE APPROACH TO COOKING FROM THE MAY FAMILY

JOY MAY

ISBN: 9780956746481

NOSH FOR STUDENTS
5TH EDITION PHOTO WITH EVERY RECIPE
A FUN STUDENT COOKBOOK

OVER 300,000 STUDENT NOSH BOOKS SOLD   JOY MAY

ISBN 9780993260933

NOSH FOR STUDENTS
VOL.2
THE SEQUEL TO 'NOSH FOR STUDENTS' ...BUT THE OTHER ONE FIRST!

OVER 300,000 STUDENT NOSH BOOKS SOLD   JOY MAY

ISBN: 9780956746467

VEGETARIAN NOSH FOR STUDENTS
2ND EDITION PHOTO WITH EVERY RECIPE
A FUN STUDENT COOKBOOK

OVER 300,000 STUDENT NOSH BOOKS SOLD   JOY MAY

ISBN 9780993260940

NOSH FOR BUSY MUMS & DADS
WITH THE HELP OF REAL KIDS, IN REAL HOMES
A FAMILY COOKBOOK WITH EVERYDAY FOOD FOR REAL FAMILIES

AUTHOR OF BEST SELLING COOKBOOK 'NOSH FOR STUDENTS'   JOY MAY

ISBN: 9780956746443

Contents

letter from Joy...

For some, life is always going to be busy, juggling work, school runs, family, leisure and so on. To help all of us, I have written a book of simple QUICK & EASY recipes, recipes that can be made with the minimum of fuss, many in as little as 20-30 minutes.

Even though the recipes are quick, I have, wherever possible, sought to always use fresh ingredients and avoid processed foods with additives and preservatives.

There are many occasions when we are short of time. I have a section in the book for when we get back home from work, where speed is most important. Also there are quick snacks for the weekend and quick meals for when we have our friends around.

Even though I am cooking every day, trying out new ingredients and combinations, I am always looking for ways to save time and to make things easier. In this book, I pass on tips and ideas that I have picked up along the way that have helped me.

I hope that you will find this book useful and something that takes the hassle out of cooking.

Enjoy.

Joy

P.S. I love to see how people are getting on with my recipes. Why not tweet a photo of your plate using "#noshbooks". I'll be watching out for it!

Our QUICK & EASY Philosophy

This book sums up our whole approach to cooking, in that it should be straightforward and down to earth. We found that people loved our approach in "Nosh for Students", our cookbook aimed at university students. In fact, many mums and grans, when buying one for others, told us that they bought one for themselves as well. This got us thinking, what is it about that book that appealed to so many different people? We believe that it is the 'no-fuss' cooking that people like. This is summed up in the way we measure ingredients with a simple mug, rather than weighing scales and measuring jugs.

We have always looked for ways to make recipes clear and easy to follow. Our approach doesn't require lots of kitchen gadgets and doesn't leave your kitchen looking as though you have been visited by a bull in a bad mood! We realise that the cooking process includes the clear up at the end and so we try to keep the pots, pans and utensils to a minimum. In fact, we have rejected recipes for this book purely on how many pans they used.

One of the main challenges of quick cooking has nothing to do with how fast you can dice an onion, or the speed with which you can skip around the kitchen whilst balancing multiple pans on the hob. It's all about quick flavour. Normally, the longer you cook things the more opportunity flavours have to develop. So does quick cooking mean flavourless meals? Certainly not. 'Quick cooking' means we just have to use ingredients that are packed with flavour from the off and using cooking methods that seal in flavour very quickly.

For us, QUICK & EASY means either quick prep and in the oven, or quick prep and on the table, always using easy to follow, hassle-free recipes.

Weapons of choice for
QUICK & EASY cooking

I am not going to give you an exhaustive list of every kitchen utensil you might possibly need. Instead, I am just going to suggest a few things that help when trying to cook QUICK & EASY food. I am not one for lots of gadgets in the kitchen; they take up space and end up gathering dust.

2 non-stick frying pans
A frying pan is a super-quick way of getting instant heat and flavour into food. There are a number of occasions when, to speed things up, it is good to have two frying pans working alongside each another.

Food processor
If you have one, USE IT. Keep it on the surface, as it makes big jobs small.

Mug
Simplicity itself. Used for simple measurements where speed is paramount and exactness isn't necessary.

Re-usable, silicon baking sheets
Stop things sticking during oven-roasting and much quicker to wash up afterwards. I have a few of them, cut to size to fit the baking tins and trays which I use the most. It saves getting out the greaseproof paper and cutting it to size, just for that one meal.

A knife sharpener
We always recommend a good, sharp knife, but there is no point having a nice knife if you don't sharpen it. A cheap knife, kept sharp, is better than a brilliant knife, left to go dull.

STOP | AUTO | PULSE

magimix

QUICK & EASY Flavours

In a QUICK & EASY book, we have talked about the need to use ingredients that are packed with instant, fresh flavour. Here are some ideas on achieving this.

Freshly ground salt and black pepper

If you have a big tub of table salt in your cooking cupboard, use it for gritting your outside path this winter, or relegate it right away to your cleaning cupboard for soaking up red wine spills on carpets. It is, by no means, the best thing for cooking. Freshly ground sea salt and freshly ground black pepper are a world apart from their pre-ground cousins.

Oil

There are all sorts of oils for all sorts of purposes, but these three oils should get you on your way to great tasting food, fast.

Extra virgin olive oil - we use it in our dressings and it's packed with flavour.

Virgin olive oil - slightly lighter in colour than extra virgin olive oil and is perfect for using in cooking, as it handles higher temperatures better.

Toasted sesame oil - is great in oriental dishes and has a lovely, delicate taste.

Herbs

I have used a lot of fresh herbs in these recipes. Dried herbs are OK in slow cook food as they have time to soak, but in quick cooking, freshness is really important. The cheapest way to get them is to have pots growing on the windowsill in your kitchen. I buy them from the supermarket and, if I remember to water them, they will keep for a few weeks and keep on growing. In the summer, I grow them outside, but using plants from a garden centre which have been accustomed to the outdoors. I have not, as yet, been successful with basil outside; I still keep that herb inside in the summer.

Most frequently used herbs:
basil
coriander
parsley
rosemary

Fresh chillies

Fresh chillies are a great way to get some instant heat in a dish, with a much fresher taste than using a teaspoon of chilli powder. I use the fat, red chillies as the tiny ones tend to be very hot. I always take the seeds out. If you have small children, don't cut the chillies too finely; that way you can just pick them out from the kids' plates. Add chillies towards the end of the cooking time as, the longer they are cooked, the hotter they become.

Lemons and Limes

Lemons and Limes should become part of your staple, weekly shop. They keep well in the fridge and are great to be able to make a salad dressing at a moment's notice, or to freshen-up dishes with a simple squeeze before serving. Both sharp and sweet at the same time, they add heaps of flavour, fast.

Honey

I love using honey, as you will notice. It is great in dressings, along with lime or lemon, but I also like to use it on fried chicken, fish and meats. It is often added at the last minute, so as not to get burned. Honey is much healthier than processed sugar and gives an immediate, rounded flavour.

Tomatoes

I have used fresh tomatoes in many recipes where you may think it would be easier just to open a tin of chopped tomatoes. However, in many cases, it is really worth the time to chop 6 tomatoes roughly to give a wonderful, fresh taste. Also, there is no need to add the teaspoon of sugar, which can be necessary when using tinned tomatoes.

So, there is my simple list of flavour-boosting ingredients. They are not wildly expensive, but can transform your cooking with ease. Enjoy.

What is quicker than just grabbing a mug and filling it! What is easier to remember as a unit of measure than a mug of this or 2 mugs of that!

Throughout the book, I have used a mug to measure ingredients. This mug holds 1/2 a pint or 300ml of liquid and is the exact size of the mug pictured opposite. So find a mug that measures up to this one and you won't go far wrong.

This book is designed so that you don't need to use any weighing scales or measuring jugs, just our mug and a few spoons. However, for those who like precision, we have included grams and millilitres too.

The mug opposite is the same one I used when writing my first book back in 2000, and it has, therefore, a place in my heart. Although it is now cracked, it still has a special spot in our mug cupboard!

a mug =

ACTUAL SIZE

SNACKS

Want a quick snack, but not a sandwich? Here are some great ideas. Ideal for weekend lunches, special breakfasts, or even a quick evening meal. The 'Salmon Tortillas' and 'East End Salad' are two of my favourites.

Cajun Chicken Pannini

Spicy chicken, gooey cheese and grilled avocado - what more can you say?

2 tablespoons **Cajun seasoning**

2 **chicken breasts**

1 tablespoon **olive oil**

2 small **ciabatta** loaves, cut in half and sliced horizontally

2 tablespoons **mayo**

2 **tomatoes**, sliced

1 large **avocado**, peeled and sliced

300g **mozzarella cheese**

1 Put the Cajun seasoning on a plate and press the chicken breasts into it, so that it is evenly distributed.

2 Heat the oil in a frying pan and fry the chicken breasts on a fairly high heat for 2 minutes each side. Turn down the heat and fry for 4 minutes each side, with a lid on the pan. Take care not to burn the Cajun seasoning.

3 Take the chicken out of the pan and leave to rest for a couple of minutes. Slice into thin strips.

4 Toast the ciabatta lightly under the grill. Spread the toasted bread with mayo and arrange the chicken, tomatoes and avocado on the bread.

5 Pull apart the mozzarella and place over the top. Put under the grill for 4–5 minutes, or until the cheese begins to bubble and go brown.

6 Enjoy!

Pork & Apple Burgers

If you have leftovers, these burgers are great to eat cold, with the sauce and a little salad.

Burgers

1 **onion**, grated

1 **Braeburn apple**, grated

500g **minced pork**

1 slice **wholemeal bread**, made into breadcrumbs

1 tablespoon **olive oil**

Sauce

2 tablespoons **mayo**

1/4 **cucumber**, grated

2 **gherkins**, finely chopped

juice of 1/2 **lemon**

salt and **pepper**

4 burger **buns**

lettuce

1 Squeeze out the excess liquid from the grated onion and apple. Mix together the apple, onion, pork, bread with salt and pepper until the ingredients are evenly distributed. Form 4 burgers.

2 Heat the oil in a frying pan and fry the burgers on a medium heat for about 10 minutes, turning frequently to prevent burning. Check to make sure they are cooked throughout.

3 Meanwhile, mix together the sauce ingredients.

4 Place each one in a bun, together with the lettuce and some of the sauce.

🌐 See some Mediterranean Lamb Burgers online:
www.noshbooks.com/lamb-burger

Prawn & Pea Salad with Tarragon & Mint

Fresh and delicious and so quick to make. This makes an excellent summer salad.

Salad

2 mugs **frozen peas**, defrosted

500g **cooked prawns**

6 **spring onions**, chopped

2 **little gem lettuces,** sliced

2 tablespoons **fresh tarragon,** chopped

2 tablespoons **fresh mint**, chopped

Dressing

4 tablespoons **mayo**

juice of a **lemon**

2 tablespoons **olive oil**

salt and **pepper**

1 Cook the peas in boiling water for 2 minutes. Drain and rinse under cold water.

2 Mix together the dressing ingredients.

3 Arrange the salad ingredients on 2 plates. Drizzle the dressing over the top.

Smoked Salmon Muffins with a Herby Bechamel Sauce

Sauce

125g **butter**, measure using packet

1 tablespoon **plain flour**

1 mug **milk**

1 tablespoon chopped, **fresh parsley**

1 tablespoon chopped, **fresh chives**

4 **breakfast muffins**

120g pack **smoked salmon**

4 **eggs**

1 To make the sauce, melt the butter in a saucepan, add the flour and cook together for 30 seconds. Add the milk and bring back to the boil, stirring frequently. Add the herbs and mix. Leave to one side until needed.

2 Cut each muffin in half, horizontally, and toast. Butter the muffins and divide the smoked salmon between them.

3 Poach the 4 eggs, drain and place on top of the smoked salmon.

4 Reheat the sauce and pour over the top.

⊙ Poaching eggs can be tricky. Here is how we do it: www.noshbooks.com/poach

Paprika Salmon Tortillas

Tortillas are an excellent and quick container for many kinds of snack food. The packet of tortillas you buy will probably say to heat them in the microwave. As an alternative, you can brush them lightly with oil and quickly fry them in a frying pan, to wake them up a bit.

Gluten-free: make sure the tortillas are gluten-free.

Dressing
4 tablespoons **Greek yoghurt**
1/4 **cucumber**, grated
juice of 1/2 **lime**

1 tablespoon **paprika**
salt and **pepper**
4 small **salmon steaks**
1 tablespoon **olive oil**

1 **red cos lettuce**
150g **cherry tomatoes**, halved
handful **fresh coriander**, roughly chopped
4 **corn tortillas**

1 Mix together the dressing ingredients and season.

2 Put the paprika and salt and pepper on a plate and mix. Press the salmon steaks into the mixture. Heat the oil in a frying pan and fry the steaks until the are nicely browned on each side; should take 2–3 minutes each side, depending on the thickness of the steak. Remove from the pan and gently flake.

3 Arrange everything on the tortillas. Serve open or rolled.

Asian Spiced Burgers with Mango Salsa & Naan 'Buns'

Try Peshwari naans if you like things a little sweeter. If you have any of the mango salsa left, you can use it with other burgers or cooked meats.

Burgers

500g **minced beef**

1 **onion**, grated and liquid squeezed out

2 cloves **garlic**, finely chopped

1 tablespoon freshly grated **ginger**

1 tablespoon **garam masala**

salt and **pepper**

1–2 tablespoons freshly chopped **coriander**

1 tablespoon **olive oil**

Mango Salsa

1 **mango** peeled and chopped

3 **spring onions**, chopped

1 **fat red chilli**, finely chopped

2 tablespoons freshly chopped **mint**

1 tablespoon freshly chopped **coriander**

zest and juice of a **lime**

1 **Romaine lettuce**

4 small **naan breads**

1 Mix together the burger ingredients in a bowl (apart from the oil). Form into 4 burgers.

2 Heat the oil in a frying pan and add the burgers. Cook on a medium heat for about 10 minutes, turning every now and then. Check one burger to make sure they are cooked through.

3 Meanwhile, mix together the salsa ingredients.

4 Serve the burgers with the lettuce, naans and the salsa.

Get out all the ingredients before you start; it makes cooking a lot calmer.

Smoked Haddock Rosti with Crème Fraîche Dressing

Rosti makes a good breakfast or snack meal. The addition of the smoked haddock makes it almost a main meal. It is inexpensive and has a distinctive flavour.

3 medium **potatoes**, grated

300g **smoked haddock**, finely sliced

1 tablespoon **olive oil**

rocket salad

Dressing

4 tablespoons **crème fraîche**

juice of a **lemon**

1 tablespoon freshly chopped **parsley** or **basil**

rocket salad

1 Squeeze the moisture out of the potatoes. Place in a bowl with the haddock and season well. Mix everything together.

2 Heat the oil in a large frying pan. Place about 1/8th of the mixture at a time in the pan and press down to flatten. Fry on a medium heat until browned on the bottom. Gently turn each rosti over to brown on the other side. They should take approximately 6–8 minutes to cook through.

3 Mix the dressing ingredients together, season, and serve everything together.

Corn Cakes with Avocado Salad

Dressing

juice of a **lime**
2 tablespoons **olive oil**
salt and **pepper**
1 teaspoon **sugar**

Corn Cakes

2 **eggs**
3/4 mug/100g **self-raising flour**
1 tablespoon **crème fraîche**
325g can **sweetcorn**, drained
bunch **spring onions**, chopped
1 dessertspoon freshly chopped **basil**
1 dessertspoon freshly chopped **chives**

2 tablespoons **olive oil**
4 slices bread or a small
ciabatta loaf, sliced

Salad

1 **avocado**, cut into small chunks
1 bag **salad leaves**
4 **tomatoes**
2 tablespoons **olive oil**

1 Mix the dressing ingredients together.

2 Beat together the eggs and flour. Add the crème fraîche and the drained sweetcorn, spring onions and herbs and mix well. Season with salt and pepper.

3 Heat the 2 tablespoons of oil in a large frying pan. Add the bread and fry on both sides until browned. Cut into strips or croutons.

4 Add the corn mixture to the frying pan, 1 tablespoon at a time, and cook on a medium heat until browned on both sides and cooked through.

5 Mix the salad ingredients together and serve the corn cakes on top. Drizzle the dressing over the salad.

🌐 We have a 'Courgette Fritters' recipe online:
www.noshbooks.com/fritters

Pastrami on Rye Salad

This is a take on the American 'Pastrami on Rye', but made into a gorgeous salad. If you are not keen on the gherkins, then you can replace them with normal cucumber.

Gluten-free: use a good, nutty gluten-free bread, instead of the rye.

Croutons

1 tablespoon **olive oil**

3 slices **rye bread**

Dressing

3 tablespoons **olive oil**

juice of a **lime**

1/2 teaspoon **sugar**

salt and **pepper**

Salad

250g **cherry tomatoes,** halved

6 **gherkins**, sliced

4 **celery sticks**, sliced

1 tablespoon roughly chopped **basil**

1 tablespoon freshly chopped **parsley**

6 **spring onions**, chopped

1 bag **salad leaves**

6 **spring onions**

120g **pastrami**

1 Heat 1 tablespoon oil in a large frying pan and add the slices of rye bread. Fry until browned on both sides. Take out of the pan and cut into croutons.

2 Mix the dressing ingredients together in a bowl.

3 Mix the salad ingredients and croutons together in a large bowl. Divide the mixture between 4 plates. Sprinkle over the dressing.

4 Arrange the pastrami on top and serve.

Tuna Niçoise

A 'Tuna Niçoise' would normally have new potatoes in it, but we thought we would mess with the old classic and see how it went. We liked it, so here it is.

Gluten-free: use gluten-free pasta.

---

4 **eggs**

2 mugs/250g **fusilli pasta**

200g **green beans**

Dressing

juice of a **lemon**

4 tablespoons **mayo**

2 tablespoons **olive oil**

salt and **pepper**

1 teaspoon **sugar**

Salad

2 x 185g tins **tuna**

30 **olives**

12 **anchovies**

6 **spring onions**, chopped

250g **cherry tomatoes**, halved

1 tablespoon freshly chopped **basil**

1 Boil the eggs for 7 minutes and run under cold water until the eggs are cool enough to handle. Gently peel and set to one side until needed.

2 Cook the pasta and add the green beans for the final 5 minutes of cooking. Drain, rinse under the cold tap and return to the pan.

3 Mix together the dressing ingredients.

4 Arrange the salad between the 4 plates and drizzle over the dressing.

🌀 Never wait for water to boil in a pan. Boil the water in the kettle first.

Potage Malakoff

An all-time famous French origin soup with wholesome vegetables and tomatoes.

1 tablespoon **olive oil**

1 **onion**, sliced

1 clove **garlic**, finely chopped

1 **potato**, cut into chunks

1 large **carrot**, sliced

4 large **tomatoes**, chopped

4 mugs boiling **water** +
2 **veg stock cubes**

2 teaspoons **Marmite**

100g chopped fresh **spinach**

1 Heat the oil in a large saucepan and fry the onion and garlic until the onion begins to soften.

2 Add the potato, carrot and tomatoes and fry for 2 minutes.

3 Add the water, stock cubes and Marmite and bring to the boil. Season well with salt and pepper and simmer for 15 minutes. Blitz the soup with a hand-held blender.

4 Add the spinach, stir through and serve. Et voilà!

🌐 Trust us, this 'Apple and Celery Soup' is a cracker:
www.noshbooks.com/apple-soup

Trout on Ciabatta
with Coriander Yoghurt Dressing

This posh 'on toast' snack is so delicious and is great if you have a few folk around for a quick lunch.

Dressing

6 tablespoons **plain yoghurt**

4 **spring** onions, finely chopped

6 **anchovy fillets**, chopped

3 tablespoons freshly chopped **coriander**

salt and **pepper**

4 **eggs**

1 tablespoon **olive oil**

400g **trout**

8 thick slices of **ciabatta** or **crusty bread**

1 clove **garlic**

1   Mix together the dressing ingredients and set to one side until needed.

2   Put the eggs in a pan of boiling water and bring to the boil, simmering for 7 minutes. Drain the boiling water away, fill the pan with cold water and leave for 2 minutes. Peel the eggs, but be careful as they will still be soft.

3   Heat the oil in a frying pan and fry the trout for about 2 minutes each side, depending on the thickness. The trout will be cooked quite quickly. Transfer to a plate, remove any skin and flake the flesh off the skin.

4   Toast the ciabatta, cut the garlic clove in half and rub the fresh garlic over the toast.

5   Serve the dressing and the trout on the ciabatta. Season with salt and pepper.

East End Salad

We called this 'East End Salad' because it is a bit like ham, egg and chips, but the spinach gives it a healthier twist.

1 tablespoon **olive oil**

4 medium **potatoes**, cut into 2cm chunks

200g pack **streaky bacon**

4 **eggs**

200g pack **baby spinach leaves**

6 **spring onions,** chopped

100g **Parmesan cheese,** shaved

Dressing

1 teaspoon **mustard**

1 tablespoon **honey**

2 tablespoons **olive oil**

juice of a **lemon**

1 Heat the oil in a large frying pan. Add the potatoes and season well with salt and pepper. Keep on a medium heat, with a lid on the pan, and fry for about 15 minutes. Keep turning the potatoes to allow them to brown on all sides.

2 Meanwhile, fry the bacon until crisp. Drain on some kitchen paper. Cut into bite-size pieces.

3 Put the eggs in boiling water and simmer for 6 minutes. Run under cold water and peel.

4 Mix together the spinach, onions and Parmesan.

5 Mix together the dressing ingredients and season. Add the spinach mixture and mix well.

6 Arrange the spinach, bacon, potatoes and eggs on plates.

Never wait for water to boil in a pan. Boil the water in the kettle first.

Panzanella Salad with Olives & Capers

Gluten-free: use gluten-free bread.

Dressing

3 tablespoons **olive oil**

1 tablespoon freshly chopped **basil**

2 tablespoons **red wine vinegar**

1 teaspoon **sugar**

salt and **pepper**

Salad

2 **ready-roasted peppers**, sliced

250g **cherry tomatoes**, or 6 **tomatoes**, cut into chunks

6 **spring onions**, sliced

20 **green olives**, halved

2 tablespoons **capers**

1 **red chilli**, chopped

bag **salad leaves**

Croutons

2 tablespoons **olive oil**

4 slices **wholemeal bread**

1 Mix together the dressing ingredients in a large bowl.

2 Add the salad ingredients and toss together. Divide between the four plates.

3 Heat the oil in a large frying pan. Add the bread and fry, on each side, until browned. Cut into croutons, sprinkle over the salad and serve.

GF V

Honey & Soy Noodles

This little noodle salad is packed with flavour. The sweetness of the honey and the richness of the egg are just wonderful together.

Gluten-free: make sure the soy sauce is gluten-free and use rice noodles.

4 nests **dried egg noodles**

200g **green beans**, cut in half

1 small **broccoli**, cut into thin strips

2 tablespoons **sesame oil**

6 **spring onions**, chopped

4 **tomatoes**, chopped

1 tablespoon freshly grated **ginger**

2 tablespoons **soy sauce**

2 tablespoons **honey**

4 **eggs**

1 Put the noodles, broccoli and green beans in a pan of boiling water and simmer for 5 minutes. Once cooked, drain and set to one side until needed.

2 Meanwhile heat 1 tablespoon of the sesame oil in a wok and fry the spring onions, tomatoes and ginger for 2 minutes. Add the soy and honey and heat through. Add the noodle mixture and mix well.

3 Put the other tablespoon of sesame oil into a frying pan and fry the 4 eggs until crispy round the edges. Serve them on top of the noodle mixture.

Roast Mushrooms Stuffed with Goats' Cheese

Gluten-free: use gluten-free bread for the breadcrumbs.

8 **portobello mushrooms**

3 tablespoons **olive oil**

1 tablespoon **balsamic vinegar**

4 **tomatoes**, sliced

2 x 120g packets of **goats' cheese**

2 slices **bread**, made into breadcrumbs

1 tablespoon **olive oil**

1 bag **mixed salad**

1   Preheat the oven to 180°C fan oven/200°C/ gas 6.

2   Take the stalks out of the mushrooms. Lightly grease a roasting tray and place the mushrooms, bottom side up, on the tray. Mix together the oil and balsamic vinegar and drizzle over the mushrooms. Season well and place in the oven for 10 minutes.

3   Take the tray out of the oven and place the sliced tomatoes and goats' cheese on top of each mushroom. Mix the breadcrumbs and the oil together and sprinkle over the mushrooms. Return to the oven for a further 10 minutes. The breadcrumbs should be lightly browned and the cheese beginning to melt.

4   Serve with the salad leaves.

If you have a food processor, USE IT! Don't keep it in a cupboard, but have it on a work surface, however small your kitchen is. It saves loads of time and energy.

GF V

Spinach & Goats Cheese Frittata

6 **eggs**

1/2 teaspoon freshly grated **nutmeg** (optional)

2 tablespoons **water**

1 tablespoon **olive oil**

1 medium **leek**, chopped

4 **spring onions**, chopped

1 **roasted red pepper** (from a jar), roughly chopped

100g pack **baby spinach**

2 **tomatoes**, sliced

125g pack **soft goats' cheese**, sliced

green salad

1 Preheat the grill.

2 Beat the eggs, nutmeg and water together and season with salt and pepper.

3 Heat the oil in a frying pan and add the leeks and onions. Fry until the leeks just begin to soften.

4 Add the peppers and spinach and fry until the spinach begins to wilt.

5 Add the egg mixture. Fry until the egg begins to set and then gently move the set egg, so that the unset egg can reach the bottom of the pan.

6 When most of the egg is set, take off the heat and add the tomatoes and goats' cheese. Place under the grill until the frittata begins to brown and rises a little.

7 Serve with salad.

🌐 We love frittatas. Here's another one:
www.noshbooks.com/sweet-potato

Minestrone Soup

2 tablespoons **olive oil**

150g **pancetta lardons**

1 **onion**, thinly sliced

1 **carrot**, peeled and cut into small cubes

2 sticks **celery**, finely sliced

1 clove **garlic**, finely chopped

400g tin **butter beans**

3 mugs/900ml **water**

2 tablespoons **tomato purée**

1 **chicken stock pot**

½ mug/100g **macaroni**

100g **fresh spinach**, roughly chopped

¼ mug freshly grated **Parmesan**

1 Heat the oil in a large saucepan and add the pancetta, onion, carrot, celery and garlic. Fry for 5 minutes, stirring frequently.

2 Add the beans, water, tomato purée, stock and macaroni. Simmer for another 5 minutes.

3 Add the spinach (you don't need to cook as it will wilt immediately in the soup).

4 Serve with the grated Parmesan over the top.

Get out all the ingredients before you start; it makes cooking a lot calmer.

Chorizo Rosti with Spinach & Poached Eggs

Rosti is quite versatile. Here, we have added some chorizo, and the flavour permeates through the potatoes. I love the egg and spinach combination. Altogether, a great meal. If you are not sure about poaching eggs, visit our website www.noshbooks.com.

Gluten-free: make sure the chorizo is gluten-free.

4 medium **potatoes**, grated

200g diced **chorizo**

1 tablespoon **olive oil**

4 **eggs**

200g **fresh spinach**

1 Squeeze the excess moisture from the grated potatoes and mix with the chorizo. Season well with salt and pepper.

2 Make 4 rosti out of the mixture. Heat the oil in a large frying pan and place the rosti in the pan. Fry on a medium heat until the potatoes are browned and cooked through. Usually takes about 10 minutes.

3 Meanwhile, poach the eggs in a frying pan half-filled with gently simmering water.

4 Once the rostis are cooked, take them out of the pan and drain on some kitchen paper. Add the spinach to the hot pan; it will wilt in about 1 minute.

5 Serve the spinach on top of the hash brown, with the egg on top.

🌐 we did a video on how to poach eggs, check it out here: www.noshbooks.com/poaching-eggs

30 MINUTES OR QUICKER

Running short on time, but still want something special to eat? All of these meals are designed with speed in mind and should be on the table in a flash.

Prawn & Chorizo Pasta

You can buy frozen prawns if you like, they are significantly cheaper and work just as well as fresh prawns in dishes like this.

Gluten-free: use rice instead of pasta and a gluten-free stock cube.

1 1/2 mugs **orzo** or **trofie pasta**

1 **chicken stock cube**

1 teaspoon **turmeric**

1 tablespoon **olive oil**

1 **red pepper**, chopped

200g **chorizo sausage**, diced

300g **cooked prawns**

6 **spring onions**, chopped

1 mug defrosted **frozen peas**

2 tablespoons freshly chopped **basil**

juice of a **lemon**

1 Put the pasta in a pan of boiling water. Add the stock cube and turmeric and mix well. Simmer for 4–5 minutes, or until the pasta is just cooked. Drain the pasta and return to the pan.

2 Heat the oil in a wok, add the peppers and fry until they begin to soften. Add the chorizo and fry until it begins to brown.

3 Add the prawns, spring onions peas, basil and pasta to the pan and heat through.

4 Squeeze over the lemon juice and season well with salt and pepper.

Balsamic Chicken with Creamy Mash

This balsamic sauce is rich and sooo yummy. Ben and Tim dipped all the spare bits of everything in it as the photograph was taken, a sure sign that it tasted good.

Gluten-free: make sure the stock cubes are gluten-free.

Mash

5 medium **potatoes**, peeled and cut into 2cm cubes

25g **butter**, measure using packet

2 tablespoons **double cream**

Balsamic Sauce

25g **butter**, measure using packet

1 tablespoon **olive oil**

2 **red onions**, sliced

1 sprig **fresh rosemary leaves**, chopped

6 tablespoons **balsamic vinegar**

2 tablespoons **runny honey**

1/2 mug **water**

1 **chicken stock cube**

1 tablespoon **olive oil**

4 **chicken breasts**

sprouting broccoli

1 Put the potatoes in boiling water, bring to the boil and then turn down to simmer for 10 minutes. Drain, return to the pan and mash with the 25g butter and cream. Season well.

2 Meanwhile, heat the butter and 1 tablespoon of oil in a saucepan and fry the onions until they begin to brown. Add the rosemary, balsamic, honey, water and stock cube. Season well, bring to the boil and then simmer for 10 minutes.

3 Heat 1 tablespoon of olive oil in a small frying pan and add the chicken breasts. Cook on a fairly high heat for 2 minutes each side. Turn down the heat to medium and fry for 4 minutes each side, with a lid on the pan. Cook for less time if the chicken breasts are small.

4 Put the sprouting broccoli in boiling water and then turn down to simmer for 4–5 minutes.

5 Serve everything together.

Penne Boscaiola

'Boscaiola' is Italian for 'woodcutter' or 'lumberjack'. He would typically gather mushrooms from the woods. This is a classic Italian dish which contains mushrooms, bacon and a creamy pasta.

Gluten-free: use gluten-free pasta.

---

3 mugs **penne pasta**

1 tablespoon **olive oil**

200g **streaky bacon**, cut into 2cm slices

6 **spring onions**, chopped

250g **chestnut mushrooms**, sliced

1 mug/300ml **single cream**

1/2 mug grated **Parmesan**

1 tablespoon freshly chopped **basil**

1 Cook the pasta in a pan of boiling, salted water. Drain and return to the pan until needed.

2 Heat the oil in a large saucepan or wok. Fry the bacon until it begins to brown.

3 Add the onions and the mushrooms and fry for 2–3 minutes.

4 Add the cream and Parmesan and season to taste. Bring to the boil.

5 Add the pasta and the chopped basil and serve immediately.

🌐 For a Pastitsio recipe, go to:
www.noshbooks.com/pastitsio

£ 1.27 /PERSON · SERVES 4 · EASE ★★☆☆☆ · PREP 20 MINS · GF OPTION

Pasta Amatriciana

Amatriciana is a classic Italian dish. It usually has bacon, tomato and basil, but here we have replaced the bacon with pancetta, which makes it a bit simpler to make.

Gluten-free: use gluten-free pasta and stock cube.

2 mugs **pasta**

2 tablespoons **olive oil**

1 **onion**, chopped

2 cloves **garlic**, finely chopped

200g **pancetta lardons**

6 **tomatoes**, roughly chopped

1/2 **fat red chilli**

2 tablespoons **tomato purée**

1/2 mug **water**

1 **vegetable stock cube**

2 tablespoons freshly chopped **basil**

1 mug grated **Parmesan cheese**

1 Cook the pasta. Once cooked, drain and return to the pan.

2 Meanwhile, heat the oil in a wok or large frying pan and add the onion and garlic. Fry until they begin to soften.

3 Add the pancetta lardons to the pan and fry until they begin to brown.

4 Add the tomatoes, chilli, tomato purée, water and stock and bring to the boil. Turn down to simmer for 5 minutes.

5 Add the pasta, basil and Parmesan and mix.

6 Serve immediately.

🐾 Never wait for water to boil in a pan. Boil the water in the kettle first.

Chorizo & Chilli Rigatoni

Chorizo has a hearty flavour which infuses pasta dishes well. I buy packets of chopped chorizo which will keep in the fridge for a week or two. This is always very handy.

Gluten-free: make sure the chorizo and pasta are gluten-free.

---

2 ½ mugs/200g **rigatoni**

1 tablespoon **olive oil**

200g **chorizo**, chopped into chunks

1 **fat red chilli**, deseeded and finely chopped

2 sprigs of **rosemary**, chopped

6 **tomatoes**, chopped into chunks

1 tablespoon **tomato purée**

4 tablespoons **crème fraîche**

½ teaspoon **sugar**

1   Put the pasta on to cook in a large saucepan. Once cooked, drain and return to the pan with a lid on.

2   Meanwhile, heat the oil in a large frying pan, or wok, and fry the chorizo for 2 minutes. Drain the excess oil from the pan.

3   Add the chilli and rosemary to the frying pan. Fry for 1 minute, being careful not to let things burn. Add the rest of the ingredients, season and stir together.

4   Add the pasta to the pan.

Olive & Tuna Pasta

Tuna can be a really handy staple to make less expensive dishes. Be careful not to stir it too much after the tuna is added, otherwise it will be a bit mushy.

Gluten-free: use gluten-free pasta and stock cube.

---

2 mugs **pasta**

1 tablespoon **olive oil**

6 **spring onions**, chopped

1 clove **garlic**, finely chopped

6 large **tomatoes**, chopped

2 tablespoons **tomato purée**

¼ mug **water**

1 **fish stock cube**

10 **black** and 10 **green olives**, roughly chopped

2 tablespoons freshly chopped **basil**

6 **anchovy fillets**, roughly chopped

2 x 185g tins **tuna**

1   Cook the pasta, drain and return to the pan.

2   Meanwhile, heat the oil in a wok or large frying pan. Fry the onions, garlic and tomatoes until they begin to soften.

3   Add the tomato purée, water and stock cube. Season well and simmer for 2 minutes.

4   Add the olives, basil, anchovies and flaked tuna, along with the cooked pasta, and mix. Heat for 1 minute.

Tarragon & Chicken Rigatoni

Tarragon can grow well outdoors, either in a pot or planted in the ground, and will keep going throughout the winter. It has a lovely aniseed/vanilla flavour, which makes this a delicious and slightly unusual dish.

Gluten-free: use gluten-free pasta and stock cube.

2 mugs **rigatoni**

50g **butter**, measure using packet

2 large **leeks**, sliced

2 cloves **garlic**, chopped

3 **chicken breasts**, cut into bite-sized pieces

250g **chestnut mushrooms**, sliced

300ml **single cream**

1 **chicken stock cube**

2 tablespoons freshly chopped **tarragon**, or 1 teaspoon of **dried tarragon**

1 Put the pasta in a pan of boiling water. Bring to the boil and then turn down to simmer for 7–8 minutes, or until the pasta is just cooked. Don't overcook. Drain and set to one side.

2 Heat the butter in a wok or large frying pan and add the leeks and the garlic. Fry on a medium heat for 3–4 minutes until the leeks begin to soften.

3 Add the chicken to the pan and cook for 3–4 minutes, until the chicken begins to brown on the outside and is no longer pink.

4 Add the mushrooms and fry for 1 minute. Add the cream, stock cube and tarragon, bring to the boil and simmer for 2 minutes. Season with salt and pepper.

5 Add the pasta to the chicken mixture.

Chicken Chilli Tortilla Pie

Obviously, if you like things really spicy you can add another chilli and use spicy tortillas. Kids will love this one. We have made it in individual dishes, but it works just as well in one big one.

Gluten-free: make sure the tortillas and stock cube are gluten-free.

1 tablespoon **olive oil**

1 **onion**, sliced

1 **clove garlic**, finely chopped

3 **chicken breasts**, cut into bite-size pieces

125g **mushrooms**, sliced

6 **tomatoes**, chopped

1/2 mug **water**

1 **chicken stock cube**

2 tablespoons **tomato purée**

1 **fat red chilli**, deseeded and chopped

175g bag **tortilla chips**

1 mug grated **Cheddar cheese**

1 Preheat the grill.

2 Heat the oil in a large frying pan or wok. Add the onion and garlic and fry until the onion begins to soften.

3 Add the chicken and fry until no longer pink.

4 Add the mushrooms and fry for 1 minute.

5 Add the tomatoes, water, stock cube, tomato purée and chilli. Bring to the boil and simmer for 5 minutes. Season with salt and pepper.

6 Pour into a casserole dish. Pile the tortilla chips on top and then the grated cheese.

7 Place under the grill for about 2 minutes. The cheese should be melted and the chips beginning to brown.

🌐 We made another tortilla pie here:
www.noshbooks.com/tortilla-pie

Spanish Prawn Risotto

Gluten-free: make sure the chorizo and stock cube are gluten-free.

2 tablespoons **olive oil**

1 **red pepper**, cut into small chunks

200g **chorizo**, cut into small chunks

2 cloves **garlic**, finely chopped

6 **tomatoes**, chopped

6 **spring onions**, sliced

1 mug **risotto rice**

2 mugs **water** + 1 tablespoonful of **concentrated liquid vegetable stock** or 1 **vegetable stock cube**

400g **raw prawns**, defrost if frozen

1 Heat the oil in a frying pan. Add the peppers and chorizo and fry until the chorizo begins to brown.

2 Add the garlic, tomatoes and onions and fry for 30 seconds.

3 Add the rice and fry until it absorbs the juices from the pan.

4 Add the water and stock and bring to the boil. Turn down to simmer for 15 minutes, or until the rice is tender.

5 Add the prawns and cook until they turn pink. Take off the heat and season with salt and pepper.

Lamb Kheema with Naan Bread

You may have heard of Kheema before in Indian restaurants, where it is a type of naan bread. Don't worry, we are not going to ask you to make naan breads! Kheema is basically a traditional Indian dish that contains lamb mince.

Gluten-free: make sure the stock cube is gluten free and serve with rice, instead of naans.

1 tablespoon **olive oil**

1 **onion**, sliced

1 tablespoon freshly grated **ginger**

1 tablespoon **fennel seeds**

1 teaspoon **cumin seeds**

1 teaspoon **tumeric**

500g **minced lamb**

2 **small sweet potatoes**, peeled and cut into 2cm chunks

2 **tomatoes**, chopped

1 mug **water** + **lamb stock cube**

3 **bay leaves**

1 mug defrosted **frozen peas**

1 **fresh chilli**, chopped

1 tablespoon freshly chopped **mint**

naan breads

1   Heat the oil in a wok or large saucepan. Add the onion and spices and fry for 1 minute.

2   Add the mince and fry until it is no longer pink.

3   Add the sweet potatoes, tomatoes, water, stock and bay leaves. Bring to the boil and then turn down and simmer for 20 minutes. Stir occasionally.

4   Add the peas, chilli and mint and heat through.

5   Serve with naan breads.

Get out all the ingredients before you start; it makes cooking a lot calmer.

Saffron Chicken & Nut Pilaf

If you do not have any saffron, just use a teaspoon of pilau rice seasoning. Delicious, mild and delicate flavour come from the nuts and saffron and little pops of sweetness come from the raisins.

pinch of **saffron** threads

25g **butter**, measure using packet

2 **onions**, chopped

3 **chicken breasts**, cut into small pieces

1 **cinnamon stick**

1 tablespoon freshly grated **ginger**

4 tablespoons **raisins** or **sultanas**

1 ½ mugs **basmati rice**

2 tablespoons **pine nuts**

2 tablespoons **cashew nuts**

1 Put the saffron (or pilau rice seasoning) in a mug of boiling water and allow to infuse.

2 Heat the butter in a wok, or large frying pan, and add the onions. Fry until they begin to soften.

3 Add the chicken and fry for 1–2 minutes until it is no longer pink. Add the mug of saffron water.

4 Add the cinnamon stick, ginger, raisins, rice and 2 more mugs of boiling water. Season well.

5 Bring everything to the boil, mixing well. Turn down to simmer for 10 minutes, with a lid or foil over the pan.

6 Sprinkle over the nuts. Put the pan on a high heat, with the lid off, and allow the mixture to get dry. Allow the bottom of the mixture to brown a little. Stir in the brown crunchy bits and then allow the next 'bottom layer' to brown. Stir again.

7 Take out the cinnamon stick and serve immediately.

Speedy Pork Bolognese

The prep for this is so quick - just pop everything in and let the food processor do all the work. If you don't have a food processor, just chop everything finely. If you don't have sun-dried tomato purée, just use regular tomato purée.

Gluten-free: use gluten-free pasta and stock cube.

1 **onion**

2 sticks **celery**

1 **carrot**

1 **red apple**, cored

1 clove **garlic**

2 tablespoons **olive oil**

500g minced **pork**

500g packet of **passata**

1 **veg stock cube**

1 tablespoon **sun-dried tomato purée**

spaghetti or **pasta**

2 tablespoons freshly chopped **parsley**

Parmesan to serve

1   Put the onion, celery, carrot, apple and garlic in a food processor and blitz until it is evenly chopped.

2   Heat the oil in a wok or large saucepan. Add the veggies and cook on a fairly high heat for 5 minutes. Keep stirring.

3   Add the mince and cook until it is no longer pink.

4   Add the passata, veg stock cube and tomato purée. Season well and simmer for 10 minutes.

5   Meanwhile, cook the spaghetti or pasta. Drain and leave to one side until needed.

6   Add the parsley to the bolognese and heat through for 30 seconds.

7   Mix the pasta and sauce together. Grate the Parmesan on top to serve.

If you have a food processor, USE IT! Don't keep it in a cupboard, but have it on a work surface, however small your kitchen is. It saves loads of time and energy.

Prawn & Spinach Risotto

Delightfully light, but tasty dish. Really quick and simple to make. The spinach is hardly cooked at all, so keeps all its glorious goodness.

2 tablespoons **olive oil**

1 **onion**, finely chopped

1 mug **risotto rice**

2 mugs **water**

2 **fish stock cubes**

450g **king prawns**

200g **spinach**, roughly chopped

1/2 mug finely grated **Parmesan**

1 Heat the oil in a wok, add the onions and fry until they begin to soften.

2 Add the rice and fry for 1 minute, to allow the rice to absorb the juices in the pan.

3 Add the water and the stock, bring to the boil and then turn down to simmer, with a lid on the pan, for 10-12 minutes, or until the rice is tender. Stir the risotto occasionally and add more water if necessary. Risotto should not be dry, but have a creamy consistency.

4 Once the rice is tender, add the prawns and the spinach and heat through for 1-2 minutes.

5 Stir in the Parmesan and season well with salt and pepper. Serve hot.

🌐 Fancy a spicy risotto? Go to:
www.noshbooks.com/risotto

Cider Sausages with Leek & Potato Mash

Excellent way of dressing up 'bangers and mash' and making it a bit more special. Use a sharp knife to cut the sausage skins, lengthways, down one side, and you will be able to easily peel them.

Gluten-free: make sure the sausages are gluten-free and you use gluten-free flour.

Mash

5 **potatoes**, peeled and cut into 2cm chunks

50g **butter**, measure using packet

3 **leeks**, sliced

1 tablespoon **olive oil**

8 **sausages**

1 **onion**, sliced

2 tablespoons **plain flour**

2 mugs **cider**

1 Simmer the potatoes for 10 minutes. Drain and return to the pan. Mash and put the lid on to keep them warm.

2 Meanwhile, heat the butter in a large frying pan and fry the leeks until they begin to brown. Add to the mashed potato and mix together. Set to one side with a lid on until needed.

3 Using the same frying pan, heat 1 tablespoon of oil. Take the skins off the sausages and pinch each one into 4 'medallions'. Fry the sausages and onion until they are browned. Remove the sausages from the pan.

4 Add the flour to the frying pan and mix. Add the cider and stir. The sauce should thicken. Put the sausages back in the pan and simmer for 2–3 minutes.

5 Season well with salt and pepper. Serve with the mash.

Mackerel in Curried Couscous Salad

Smoked mackerel has a strong, distinctive flavour. You can buy it vacuum packed and cooked, so no need to have a strong fish smell in the kitchen. Unopened, it will keep in the fridge for ages, so very handy.

2 teaspoons **Rogan Josh curry paste**

2 mugs **boiling water**

1 mug **couscous**

1/2 mug/50g **sultanas**

250g **smoked mackerel fillets**, skinned and flaked

4 **spring onions**, chopped

1/2 **red pepper**, chopped

2 **tomatoes**, chopped

1 tablespoon freshly chopped **coriander**

1/2 **cucumber**, diced

juice of a **lemon**

1 Put the curry paste in a bowl, add the boiling water and stir. Add the couscous and sultanas and cover. Leave for 5 minutes.

2 Add the rest of the ingredients and gently stir. Season with salt and pepper.

Coronation Chicken Salad

This is a take on the old fashioned 'Coronation Chicken'. It has a lovely delicate taste. The mango in the salad provides a freshness to the whole dish.

Gluten-free: make sure the curry paste is gluten-free.

Mango Rice Salad

3/4 mug **rice**

1 **mango**, peeled and cut into small dice

2 tablespoons freshly chopped **coriander**

6 **spring onions**, chopped

1 **green apple**, chopped into small pieces

2 tablespoons **toasted, flaked almonds**

Chicken

1 tablespoon **Korma curry paste**

juice of a **lemon**

3 **chicken breasts**, cut into bite-sized pieces

1 tablespoon **olive oil**

Sauce

3 tablespoons **mayo**

1 tablespoon **mango chutney**

1 tablespoon **yoghurt**

salt and **pepper**

2 tablespoons freshly chopped **coriander**

1 Put the rice in 1 1/2 mugs boiling water. Simmer for 12 minutes until tender. Take out of the pan to cool a little.

2 Mix together the rest of the mango rice salad ingredients in a bowl, season, and add the rice when it has cooled slightly.

3 Mix the curry paste, lemon juice and chicken. Heat the oil in a frying pan and fry the chicken pieces on a medium heat, until they are cooked through and nicely browned.

4 Mix together the sauce ingredients.

5 Arrange the rice and the chicken on the plates, sprinkle over the coriander and drizzle over the sauce.

Chicken, Bacon & Avocado Salad

1 tablespoon **olive oil**

8 slices **bacon**

3 **chicken breasts**

2 tablespoons **sesame seeds**

2 teaspoons **honey**

Dressing

2 tablespoons **olive oil**

juice of a **lime**

1 teaspoon **honey**

salt and **pepper**

bag **salad leaves**

250g **cherry tomatoes**, halved

1/2 **cucumber**, cut into sticks

1 **avocado**, peeled and sliced

1 Heat the oil in a frying pan and add the bacon. Cook until crispy. Remove from the pan and cut into small pieces. The bacon will almost crumble.

2 Add the chicken breasts to the pan. Season with salt and pepper. Fry for 2 minutes, each side, on a fairly high heat.

3 Turn down the heat and fry, with a lid on the pan, for 4 minutes on one side.

4 Turn over the chicken and add the sesame seeds. Fry for 2 minutes, turn over again, and distribute the sesame seeds. Add the honey and fry for 2 minutes, being careful not to burn the honey. Remove from the pan and cut into slices.

5 Mix the dressing ingredients together.

6 Arrange the salad leaves, tomatoes, cucumber and avocado on the plates. Put the chicken over the top, then the bacon, and finally drizzle with the dressing.

£ 1.03 /PERSON | SERVES 4 | EASE ★★☆☆☆ | PREP 30 MINS

Sweet Potato, Bacon & Orzo Pasta Salad

2 large **sweet potatoes**, peeled and cut into 2cm cubes

2 tablespoons **olive oil**

1 mug/250g **orzo pasta**

2 mugs defrosted **frozen peas**

200g **streaky bacon**

6 **spring onions**, chopped

1 tablespoon roughly chopped, **fresh mint**

100g **feta cheese**

1 Preheat the oven to 200°C fan oven/220°C/ gas 7.

2 Mix the sweet potatoes with the 2 tablespoons olive oil, season with salt and pepper, and place on a large baking tray. Put in the oven for 25 minutes, or until the potatoes are tender and lightly browned.

3 Meanwhile, put the pasta in boiling water and simmer for 3 minutes. Add the peas to the pan for the last 2 minutes of cooking. Drain and return to the pan.

4 Fry or grill the bacon until it is browned and crispy. Cut into bite-sized pieces.

5 Mix everything together, apart from the feta. Divide between the plates and crumble the feta over the top. Season with salt and pepper.

Sweet Chilli Chicken

Sauce

4 tablespoons **soft, brown sugar**

2 tablespoons freshly grated **ginger**

1/2 x 190ml bottle **sweet chilli sauce**

4 tablespoons **mirin** or **white wine vinegar**

juice of 2 **limes**

1/2 mug **water**

1 teaspoon **cornflour**

3 **chicken breasts**, cut into thin strips

1 1/2 mugs **basmati rice**

200g **mangetout**, cut into thin strips

1 tablespoon **olive oil**

1 **fat red chilli**, chopped (optional)

1 Mix together the sauce ingredients. Add the chicken strips and leave for 5 minutes.

2 Meanwhile, put the rice on to cook. Once it is cooked, put the mangetout on top and replace the pan lid. The mangetout will cook in the heat from the rice.

3 Heat the oil in a large frying pan or wok. Add the chicken, but not the sauce. Fry on a medium heat until the chicken is cooked; should take 4–5 minutes.

4 Add the sauce and bring to the boil. Simmer for 1 minute. Add the chilli now if you want to add a real kick.

5 Serve with the rice and mangetout.

🍴 Cook foolproof rice in 15 minutes. Put 2 mugs of boiling water in a pan and add 1 mug of basmati rice. Bring to the boil. Simmer with a lid on the pan for 12 minutes. The water should be absorbed and the rice fluffy.

£0.89 /PERSON · SERVES 4 · EASE ★★☆☆☆ · PREP 25 MINS · GF OPTION

Sausage & Trottole Pasta

A brilliant weekday alternative to the normal 'Spag Bol'. The chilli is optional if you have younger children.

Gluten-free: use gluten-free pasta, stock cube and sausages.

1 tablespoon **olive oil**

1 **red onion**, chopped

2 cloves **garlic**, chopped

500g **sausages**

1 mug **water** + 1 **vegetable stock cube**

6 medium **tomatoes**, chopped

1 tablespoon **tomato purée**

1 **fat red chilli**, sliced (optional)

2 mugs **trottole** pasta

2 tablespoons freshly chopped **basil**

1 Heat the oil in a wok, or large frying pan. Add the onion and garlic and fry until the onion begins to soften.

2 Take the skins of the sausages and break up. Add to the pan and fry until they begin to brown.

3 Add the water, stock cube, tomatoes and tomato purée. Bring to the boil and then turn down to simmer for 5 minutes. Add the chilli, if you are using it, and season well with salt and pepper.

4 Meanwhile, cook the pasta, drain and combine with the sausage mixture.

5 Sprinkle the basil over and serve.

Chicken & Mushroom Curry with Coconut Milk

This is super quick for a curry. Perfect for when you get in from work and need food on the table 'pronto'.

Gluten-free: use gluten-free plain flour in the sauce and gluten-free naan bread.

1 1/2 mugs **basmati rice**

1 tablespoon **olive oil**

1 **onion**, sliced

3 **chicken breasts**, cut into bite-sized pieces

1 tablespoon **plain flour**

4 tablespoons **Korma curry paste**

400g tin **coconut milk**

250g **mushrooms**, sliced

peshwari naan to serve

1 Put the rice on to cook in 3 mugs of boiling water. Once cooked, remove from the heat and leave with a lid on until needed.

2 Meanwhile, heat the oil in a large frying pan or wok. Add the onion and fry until it begins to soften.

3 Put the naan in the oven, see packet instructions.

4 Add the chicken to the frying pan and fry until no longer pink. Add the curry paste and mix well.

5 Add the flour and mix well.

6 Add the coconut milk and mushrooms. Bring to the boil and then turn down to simmer for 2 minutes.

🕑 Never wait for water to boil in a pan. Boil the water in the kettle first.

Basil & Parmesan Meatballs

When making the meatballs, if you have a food processor, you can make the breadcrumbs, add the onion, then the basil and the rest of the meatball contents, blitzing between each addition.

Gluten-free: use gluten-free bread in the meatballs and GF stock cube and pasta.

Tomato sauce

2 tablespoons **olive oil**

1 **onion**, finely chopped

1 clove **garlic**, chopped

6 **tomatoes**, chopped

2 tablespoons **tomato purée**

1 teaspoon **brown sugar**

1 mug **water**

1 **veg stock cube**

3 sprigs **fresh rosemary**

Meatballs

500g **beef mince**

2 slices **wholemeal bread**, made into breadcrumbs

1 **onion**, chopped

1 tablespoon freshly chopped **basil**

1/2 mug/4 tablespoons grated **Parmesan**

1 **egg**, beaten

salt and **pepper**

2 tablespoons **olive oil** to fry

tagliatelle or **spaghetti** to serve

1 To make the sauce, heat the oil in a large saucepan, add the onions and garlic and fry until the onions begin to soften.

2 Add the rest of the sauce ingredients and bring to the boil. Turn down to simmer for 15 minutes. Take out the rosemary and blitz with a hand-held blender. If you do not have one, just leave as it is.

3 Combine together the beef, breadcrumbs, onion, basil, Parmesan, egg and salt and pepper in a large bowl. Make into about 24 meatballs.

4 Heat the oil in a frying pan and add the meatballs. Cook on a medium heat until they are browned on all sides and cooked through. This may take about 10 minutes.

5 Meanwhile, cook the tagliatelli; usually takes no more than 4 minutes.

£ 1.34 /PERSON SERVES 4 EASE ★★☆☆☆ PREP 20 MINS GF OPTION

Paprika Sausage Salad

Gluten-free: use gluten-free sausages.

8 good quality **sausages**
2 teaspoons **paprika**
1 tablespoon **olive oil**

Dressing

3 tablespoons **olive oil**
2 tablespoons **cider vinegar**
1 tablespoon **runny honey**
salt and **pepper**

Salad

250g **cherry tomatoes**, each cut into 4
20 **black olives**
1 teaspoon **capers**, chopped
2 **cos lettuce**, sliced
8 **spring onions**, sliced

Parmesan cheese, shaved

1 Peel the skins off the sausages and break each one into 4 pieces; no need to roll into balls. Sprinkle the paprika onto a plate and add salt and pepper. Roll the sausage pieces in the mixture.

2 Heat the oil in a large frying pan and add the sausages. Fry until the pieces are browned and cooked through; it will take about 5 minutes.

3 Mix together the dressing ingredients.

4 Mix together the salad ingredients in a bowl. Add the dressing and mix together.

5 Serve with the sausages and Parmesan.

Cashew Nut Chicken

Gluten-free: make sure the stock cubes are gluten-free.

Cashew nut paste

1 **onion**, roughly chopped

2 tablespoons **tomato purée**

50g **cashew nuts**

1 tablespoon **garam masala**

2 **garlic** cloves

juice of 1/2 a **lemon**

1 teaspoon **turmeric**

1 mug **water**

1/2 mug **basmati rice**

50g **cashew nuts**

2 tablespoons **olive oil**

3 **chicken breasts**, cut into bite-size pieces

14 **ready-to-eat apricots**, roughly chopped

1 **chicken stock cube**

3 tablespoons **natural yoghurt**

3 tablespoons freshly chopped **coriander**

1 Put the ingredients for the nut paste in a food processor and whizz to form a paste. If you do not have a processor, simply chop everything very finely.

2 Cook the rice and then set to one side, with the lid on the pan, until needed.

3 Meanwhile, heat a wok and dry toast the second 50g cashew nuts. Keep them moving in the pan, so they don't burn. Remove from the wok and leave to one side until needed.

4 Heat the oil in a wok, add the chicken breast and fry for 1 minute.

5 Add the nut paste, apricots, stock cube and simmer for 3–4 minutes until the chicken is cooked through.

6 Mix the coriander and yoghurt together in a small bowl and serve with the chicken and rice.

Leek & Tarragon Rigatoni

It is good for us to have a veggie meal every now and again. The mushrooms in this recipe are quite substantial for those of us who have withdrawal symptoms and ask, "where is the meat?".

Gluten-free: just use gluten-free pasta.

2 mugs **rigatoni**

50g **butter**, measure using packet

1 tablespoon **olive oil**

2 large **leeks**, sliced

250g **chestnut mushrooms**

2 tablespoons freshly chopped **tarragon**, or 1 teaspoon **dried tarragon**

1 mug/300ml **single cream**

1 **veg stock cube**

¼ mug grated **Parmesan-style cheese**

1 Put the pasta on to cook. Once cooked, drain and return to the pan, with a drizzle of olive oil, until needed.

2 Meanwhile, heat the butter and oil in a wok or large saucepan. Fry the leeks until soft and beginning to brown. Add the mushrooms and fry for a further 2 minutes.

3 Add the tarragon, cream, stock and cook for 2 minutes. Season to taste.

4 Stir in the pasta and the Parmesan.

Salmon & Coriander Patties with Crème Fraîche Raita

Gluten-free: use gluten-free breadcrumbs in the patties.

Raita

3 tablespoons **crème fraîche**

1/4 **cucumber**, grated

1 tablespoon freshly chopped **chives**

4 small **salmon fillets** approx. 200g

2 slices **white bread**, made into breadcrumbs

2 teaspoons **capers**, chopped

2 tablespoons freshly chopped **coriander**

1 tablespoon **olive oil**

salad to serve

1 Mix the raita ingredients together and season to taste.

2 Put the salmon in a food processor and pulse a few times; no need to make the fish into a paste. If you don't have a processor, chop very finely.

3 Add the breadcrumbs, capers and coriander to the processor and pulse a couple of times. Season with salt and pepper.

4 Tip the mixture out onto a board and form into 8 patties.

5 Heat the oil in a frying pan and fry the patties for about 4 minutes on each side, on a medium heat.

6 Serve with the salad and raita.

£ 1.50 /PERSON SERVES 4 EASE ★★☆☆☆ PREP 25 MINS OK TO FREEZE ❄

Quick Chicken & Red Lentil Curry

1 tablespoon **olive oil**

1 **onion**, sliced

3 **chicken breasts**, cut into small pieces

2 tablespoons **Korma curry paste**

6 large **tomatoes**, chopped

1 mug **water**

1/2 mug/100g **red lentils**

100g **fresh spinach**, roughly chopped

rice and **yoghurt** to serve

1   Heat the oil in a wok or large saucepan. Add the onions and fry until they begin to soften.

2   Add the chicken and fry until it is no longer pink.

3   Add the curry paste and cook for 1 minute.

4   Add the tomatoes, water and lentils. Bring to the boil, then turn down to simmer for 15 minutes.

5   Put the rice on to cook. Set to one side until needed.

6   Stir the spinach into the curry and cook for 30 seconds.

7   Serve with the rice and yoghurt.

Marsala Mushrooms with Creamy Polenta

You can get some excellent packs of mixed mushrooms (which work well in this dish) from most supermarkets. It is well worth splashing out a little, as the variation in the types of mushroom add different textures and flavours.

Polenta

1 1/2 mugs/450ml **milk**

1 clove **garlic**, finely chopped

1/2 mug/100g **fine polenta**

1/2 mug/150ml **double cream**

1/2 mug/30g grated **Parmesan**

150g **mascarpone cheese**

50g **butter**, measure using packet

450g **mixed mushrooms**, e.g. porcini, girolles and chanterelles, roughly chopped

2 cloves **garlic**, chopped

1/4 mug **Marsala wine**

2 tablespoons freshly chopped **basil**

1 To make the polenta, put the milk, garlic, polenta, cream and salt and pepper in a medium pan. Bring to the boil, stirring frequently. Turn down to simmer for 10 minutes, again stirring frequently. Add the Parmesan and mascarpone and mix well. Set to one side until needed.

2 Meanwhile, melt the butter in a large frying pan or wok. Add the mushrooms and garlic and fry gently for 2 minutes. Season well, add the Marsala wine and cook for 1 minute. Take off the heat and add the fresh basil.

3 Serve together.

Kheema Aloo

Kheema Aloo is a traditional South Asian dish with mince and potatoes, ginger and garlic. With my limited understanding of the Indian language, basically, 'kheema' means the minced meat and 'aloo' the potatoes.

1 tablespoon **olive oil**

4 **cardamom pods**

1 **cinnamon stick**

3 **cloves**

2 **onions**, chopped

500g **minced lamb**

2 teaspoons **garam masala**

1 **fat red chilli**, finely chopped

2 cloves **garlic**, finely chopped

1 dessertspoon freshly grated **ginger**

2 medium **potatoes**, cut into small cubes

400g **tin tomatoes**

1/2 mug **water**

2 tablespoons freshly chopped **coriander**

rice or **naan** to serve

1 Heat the oil in a wok or large frying pan. Add the cardamom pods, cinnamon stick and cloves and fry for 30 seconds, to release the flavours.

2 Add the onions and fry until they begin to soften.

3 Add the lamb to the pan and fry until it is no longer pink.

4 Add the garam masala, chilli, garlic and ginger and fry for another minute. Season well with salt and pepper.

5 Add the potatoes, tomatoes and water and bring to the boil. Turn down to simmer, with a lid on the pan, for 12–15 minutes until the potatoes are tender.

6 Cook the rice or naan.

7 Stir the coriander into the meat mixture and serve with the rice or naan bread.

Harissa & Tuna Potato Salad

The harissa dressing really brings this salad alive; rich and tomatoey, with a spicy kick for good measure.

500g **new potatoes**, cut into 2cm chunks

200g **green beans**

1 mug/100g frozen **soya beans**, defrosted

2 x 185g tins **tuna**, drained and flaked

1/2 bag **rocket leaves**

8 **anchovies**, sliced lengthways

Dressing

2 teaspoons **harissa paste**

juice of a **lemon**

2 tablespoons **olive oil**

1 teaspoon **sugar**

1 Put the potatoes in a pan of boiling water, bring to the boil and then simmer for 5 minutes. Add the beans and soya beans and simmer for a further 5 minutes. Drain and return to the pan.

2 Gently stir in the flaked tuna. Serve on a bed of rocket leaves. Put a few sliced anchovies on each plate of salad.

3 Mix together the dressing ingredients and drizzle over.

🌐 Looking for a cheap and cheerful dish? Try:
www.noshbooks.com/tuna-hash

Warm Asian Salmon Salad

This is a delicious, crunchy, fresh tasting salad, which is full of barely cooked vegetables and healthy salmon. So, not only can you enjoy eating it, you can also feel totally guilt-free at the same time.

Gluten-free: make sure the soy and fish sauce are gluten-free.

2/3 mug/150g **basmati rice**

2 **pak choi**, finely sliced

100g **sugar snaps** or **mangetout**, halved

3 tablespoons **sesame oil**

4 **salmon fillets**

3 tablespoons **sesame seeds**

6 **spring onions**, sliced

3 tablespoons **dark soy sauce**

2 teaspoons **Thai fish sauce**

juice of a **lime**

1 tablespoon **honey**

100g **bean sprouts**

2 tablespoons freshly chopped **coriander**

1 Add the rice to 1 1/3 mugs of boiling water and simmer gently for 12 minutes. Take the pan off the heat and add the pak choi and sugar snaps. Replace the lid and leave to steam.

2 Heat the sesame oil in a large frying pan and fry the salmon until browned and cooked through.

3 Add the sesame seeds and spring onions and cook gently until they begin to brown.

4 Add the soy, fish sauce, lime and honey. Cook on a low heat for 30 seconds, being careful not to burn the honey.

5 Take the fish out and add the beansprouts, cooked rice, sugar snaps, pak choi and coriander and heat through for 1 minute.

6 Flake the fish and gently stir into the rice mix. Serve immediately.

Sausage & Bean Soup

This is a hearty soup, full of goodness. A meal in one pot.

Gluten-free: make sure the sausages and stock are gluten-free.

8 **sausages**

1 tablespoon **olive oil**

1 **onion**, sliced

3 **celery sticks**, thinly sliced

2 cloves **garlic**, finely chopped

500g **passata**

1 **chicken stock pot**

2 mugs/600ml **water**

400g tin **cannellini beans**

100g **fresh spinach**, roughly chopped

1 Cut the sausage skins lengthways and peel off the skins. Squeeze each one into 6 pieces. Heat the oil in a large saucepan pan or wok. Fry the sausages until they are browned on all sides. Remove from the pan.

2 Add the onion, celery and garlic to the pan and fry until everything is lightly browned.

3 Add the passata, stock, water and beans. Return the sausages to the pan and season well with salt and pepper. Bring to the boil and then simmer for 5 minutes.

4 Take off the heat and add the spinach to the pan. Stir together and the spinach will wilt.

Italian Cod & Bean Stew

Italian fish stew with a hint of spice. Find some good crusty bread to serve with this dish.

Gluten-free: make sure the fish stock cubes are gluten-free.

1 tablespoon **olive oil**

1 **red pepper**, chopped

4 slices **streaky bacon**, chopped

6 **spring onions**, chopped

6 **tomatoes**, roughly chopped

2 cloves **garlic**, finely chopped

2 teaspoons **paprika**

1 pinch of **saffron**

400g tin **cannellini beans**, drained and washed

1 mug **water** + 1 **fish stock cube**

4 **cod steaks**, cut into bite-sized pieces

2 tablespoons freshly chopped **coriander**

crusty bread to serve

1 Heat the oil in a large frying pan or wok. Add the pepper and bacon and fry until it begins to brown. Season well with salt and pepper.

2 Add the spring onions, tomatoes and garlic and fry for 1 minute.

3 Add the paprika, saffron, beans, water and stock and bring to the boil. Add the cod and simmer gently for 3-4 minutes, or until the fish is cooked.

4 Add the chopped coriander and stir in. Serve with some crusty bread.

Five Spice Pork with Ginger & Honey

This has a real 'takeaway" feel, but with fresh ingredients and no additives. It is, at least, half the price and also much quicker than waiting for the takeaway!

Gluten-free: make sure the soy sauce is gluten-free.

1 1/2 mugs **basmati rice**

2 teaspoons **cornflour**

3 teaspoons **5 spice powder**

4 **pork steaks**, thinly sliced

2 tablespoons **toasted sesame oil**

1 **green or red pepper**, chopped

6 **spring onions**, chopped

2 tablespoons freshly grated **ginger**

Sauce

1 mug **water**

1 tablespoon **cornflour**

2 tablespoons **mirin**

2 tablespoons **soy**

juice of 1/2 **lime**

2 tablespoons **honey**

1   Put the rice on to cook in 3 mugs of boiling water. Mix the sauce ingredients together.

2   Mix the cornflour and 5 spice powder and place on a plate. Roll the pork slices in the mixture, making sure to cover all the pork. Season with salt and pepper.

3   Heat the oil in a wok and fry the pork for 1-2 minutes. Remove from the pan as soon as the pork is cooked through.

4   Add the peppers to the pan and fry for 1 minute. Add the onions and ginger and fry for a further minute.

5   Mix the sauce ingredients together and add to the pan. Return the pork to the pan, bring to the boil and simmer for 1 minute.

6   Serve with the rice.

Mushroom & Bacon Tagliatelle

Gluten-free: use gluten-free pasta.

2 mugs pasta/4 bunches **tagliatelle**

250g **streaky bacon**

1 tablespoon **olive oil**

1 **yellow/orange pepper**, cut into small chunks

2 cloves **garlic**, finely chopped

bunch **spring onions**, chopped

250g **chestnut mushrooms**, sliced

300ml **Greek yoghurt**

1/2 mug/50g **pine nuts**

2 tablespoons freshly chopped **basil**

1 Put the pasta on to cook. Once cooked, drain and return to the pan until needed.

2 Meanwhile, fry or grill the bacon until browned. Cut into bite-sized pieces.

3 Heat the oil in a large frying pan, or wok, and add the peppers and garlic. Fry for 2-3 minutes until the peppers begin to brown. Add the mushrooms and spring onions and fry for 1 minute.

4 Add the yoghurt and pine nuts and heat through.

5 Add the bacon, basil and pasta to the pan and mix together. Season well.

Never wait for water to boil in a pan. Boil the water in the kettle first.

£ 1.36 /PERSON · SERVES 4 · EASE ★★★★☆ · PREP 25 MINS

Almonds & Apricot Chicken Tagine

Tagines typically sit in the oven for long periods of time which, if you have got the time, is great. Most people want things a little quicker though, so we wanted to try and get the flavour without all that time. This one is packed with fruity flavours and the unmistakable spices of a tagine, in a fraction of the time.

Couscous

1 mug **couscous**

2 mugs **boiling water**

1 **vegetable stock cube**

2 tablespoons freshly chopped **coriander**

1 tablespoon **olive oil**

1 large **onion**, sliced

2 cloves **garlic**, finely chopped

3 **chicken breasts**, cut into bite-sized pieces

1 teaspoon ground **cinnamon**

1 **cinnamon stick**

1 teaspoon **ground coriander**

1/2 teaspoon **paprika**

1 mug/175g **ready-to-eat dried apricots**, roughly chopped

250g **mushrooms**, sliced

1 mug/175g **sultanas**

1 1/2 mugs **water** + 1 **chicken stock cube**

2 teaspoons **cornflour**

handful freshly chopped **coriander**

50g **flaked almonds**

1 Put the couscous in a large bowl, add the boiling water and stock cube and stir well, to dissolve the stock. Cover the bowl with a plate, or cling film, and leave to one side for at least 4 minutes. Just before serving, add the fresh coriander.

2 Heat the oil in a large frying pan or wok. Add the onions and garlic and fry until they begin to soften.

3 Add the chicken and fry until no longer pink.

4 Add the cinnamon, cinnamon stick, ground coriander, paprika, apricots, mushrooms, sultanas, water and stock. Bring to the boil and turn down to simmer for 10 minutes.

5 Mix the cornflour with a little water and add to the pan. This should thicken the sauce.

6 Just before serving, stir in the fresh coriander. Serve with the couscous and sprinkle over the flaked almonds.

QUICK PREP, THEN POP IT IN THE OVEN

If you have a little more time, but don't want to be standing in the kitchen for ages, try some of these "quick prep" recipes. Just pop them in the oven to cook, while you get on with other important things.

Sausage & Mash with Cumberland Sauce

Gluten-free: use gluten-free plain flour in the gravy and gluten-free sausages and stock cubes.

12 good quality **sausages**

1 tablespoon **olive oil** to fry

4-5 medium **potatoes**

3 tablespoons **cream** or 50g **butter**, measure using packet

Cumberland Sauce

1 tablespoon **olive oil**

1 **onion**, sliced

1 tablespoon **plain flour**

1/2 mug **Marsala wine** (or **sherry**)

zest of a **lemon**

2 tablespoons **blackcurrant jelly (jam)**

1 mug **water** + 1 **beef stock cube**

1 Preheat the oven to 180°C fan oven/200°C/ gas 6. Put the sausages on a roasting tray and sprinkle with oil and salt and pepper. Place in the oven for 40 minutes.

2 Peel the potatoes and cut into 2cm chunks. Place in boiling water and then simmer for 10 minutes. Drain and return to the pan. Mash with the cream, or butter, and season with salt and pepper. Set to one side until needed.

3 Meanwhile, make the sauce. Heat the oil in a frying pan and fry the onion until it begins to soften. Add the flour and cook for 30 seconds, mixing thoroughly. Add the rest of the ingredients and bring to the boil. The sauce should thicken slightly. Simmer for 2–3 minutes.

4 Serve the potatoes and sauce with the sausages.

Oven-Baked Sausage Roast

500g **sausages**

1 **onion**, cut into wedges

125g **mushrooms**, sliced

2 cloves **garlic**, finely chopped

1 **red** and 1 **yellow pepper**, cut into small chunks

250g **cherry tomatoes**

2 tablespoons **balsamic vinegar**

2 tablespoons **olive oil**

Garlic bread

50g softened **butter**, measure using packet

2 cloves **garlic**

1 tablespoon freshly chopped **basil** or **parsley**

salt and **pepper**

1 **french stick** or **baguette**

1 Preheat the oven to 180°C fan oven/200°C/ gas 6.

2 Take the skins off the sausages by just slitting them with a knife. The skins should peel off quite easily. Squeeze each one into 4 or 5 pieces.

3 Place the sausages on a large roasting tray, along with the rest of the ingredients, apart from the garlic bread. Mix everything together and season. Place in the oven for 45 minutes.

4 Meanwhile, mix together the butter, garlic, and basil and season. Cut slices into the bread stick, but not right through. Place the bread stick on a large piece of foil and gently poke the butter mix into the slits you have made in the bread.

5 Wrap the bread in the foil and place in the oven for the last 20 minutes of the cooking time.

6 Serve everything together.

Meatball Pasta Bake

Gluten-free: use gluten-free bread, pasta and stock cube.

3 mugs **pasta**

Meatballs

500g minced **beef**

1 **egg**

1 teaspoon **dried oregano**

2 slices **bread**, made into breadcrumbs

salt and **pepper**

1 tablespoon olive **oil**

Sauce

1 **onion**, chopped

2 **ready-roasted red peppers** (from a jar), roughly chopped

500g **passata**

1/2 mug **water** + 1 **beef stock cube**

200g **mozzarella cheese**

1 tablespoon **fresh thyme leaves**, chopped

1 Put the pasta on to cook. Drain and return to the pan until needed.

2 Meanwhile, make the meatballs. Mix the mince, egg, oregano and 1/2 the breadcrumbs together in a bowl. Season well with salt and pepper. Divide into 24 pieces and form the meatballs.

3 Heat the oil in a large frying pan, or wok, and fry the meatballs until they are cooked through and browned on all sides. Place in the casserole dish.

4 To make the sauce, add the onions to the pan and fry until they begin to soften.

5 Add the peppers, passata, water and stock cube and simmer for 2 minutes.

6 Mix in the drained pasta and pour into the casserole dish with the meatballs.

7 Pull apart the mozzarella and spread over the top, along with the thyme. Sprinkle over the rest of the breadcrumbs. Place under the grill for 5 minutes. The cheese should be bubbling and the breadcrumbs browned.

🌐 You can't beat a good old pasta bake. Here is another: www.noshbooks.com/tuna-bake

Quick Beef & Yorkshire Pudding

This is Ron's Yorkshire Pudding recipe. Even though he does not originate from Yorkshire, and I do, he makes the best 'Yorkshires' in our house. This makes a fun meal to share.

Yorkshire Pudding

1 mug **plain flour**

5 **eggs**

5 tablespoons **milk**

pinch of **salt**

2 tablespoons **Trex** or **White Flora**

Beef

1 tablespoon **olive oil**

1 **red onion**, chopped

750g **minced beef**

2 tablespoons **plain flour**

2 mugs/600ml **water**

2 **beef stock pots**

4 **carrots**, cut into small dice

2 sprigs **rosemary**

green veg

1   Preheat the oven to 250°C fan oven/270°C/gas 9. Leave only one shelf in the oven to allow the pudding plenty of room to rise.

2   Mix the Yorkshire Pudding ingredients to a smooth consistency. Add 5 tablespoons of water, enough to make the mixture as thick as single cream. Store in a cool place until needed.

3   On the hob, heat the Trex in a large hob to oven casserole dish, preferably one which is wide and shallow. When the fat begins to smoke a little, add the beaten-up Yorkshire pudding mix. Leave on a high heat and do not stir. Once the Yorkshire begins to slightly brown around the edges carefully transfer into the hot oven and bake for about 20 minutes. The pudding should rise and be quite brown. Don't open the oven until you are sure it is done.

4   Meanwhile, prepare the beef. Heat the oil in a large frying pan or wok, add the onions and fry until they begin to soften. Add the mince and fry until it is no longer pink.

5   Add the flour and mix well. Add the rest of the ingredients and season with salt and pepper. Bring to the boil and then turn down to simmer for 15 minutes.

6   Meanwhile, put the green veg on to cook.

Chorizo Pasta Bake

As an alternative, you could replace the Cheddar cheese with Parmesan, or even mozzarella.

Gluten-free: make sure the chorizo and pasta are gluten-free.

2 tablespoons **olive oil**

2 **red peppers**, roughly chopped

2 **courgettes**, cubed

300g **chorizo sausage**, cut into chunks

2 mugs **pasta**

6 **tomatoes**, chopped

1/2 mug **water**

1 tablespoon **tomato purée**

1 clove **garlic**, finely chopped

1 tablespoon freshly chopped **basil**

15 **olives**, halved

1 mug grated **Cheddar cheese**

1 Heat the oil in a wok and add the peppers and courgettes. Fry until they begin to brown. Add the chorizo and fry until it begins to brown.

2 Cook the pasta, drain and set to one side until needed.

3 Add the tomatoes, water, tomato purée, garlic and basil to the wok. Bring to the boil and then turn down to simmer for 5 minutes.

4 Preheat the grill.

5 Add the pasta, basil and olives to the wok. Mix everything and then pour into a flameproof casserole dish. Sprinkle the cheese over the top and place under the grill for about 5 minutes to brown the top.

🌐 See another pasta bake online:
www.noshbooks.com/pasta-bake

Lamb & Chilli Gratinata

Good, inexpensive midweek dish. You could exchange the passata for a tin of tomatoes and a tablespoon of tomato purée, if you like.

Gluten-free: use gluten-free pasta, stock cube and breadcrumbs.

2 mugs **penne pasta**

1 tablespoon **olive oil**

1 **onion**, chopped

500g **lamb mince**

2 cloves **garlic**, finely chopped

150g **mushrooms**, sliced

1/2 **red chilli**, deseeded and chopped

500g jar of **passata**

1/2 mug **water**

1 lamb **stock cube**

75g **olives**, about 20

100g **fresh spinach**, roughly chopped

2 slices **wholemeal bread** made into breadcrumbs

200g **mozzarella cheese**, pulled apart

1 Preheat the oven to 180°C fan oven/200°C/gas 6. Grease a large casserole dish.

2 Cook the pasta. Drain, return to the pan and set to one side.

3 Meanwhile, heat the oil in a large frying pan, or wok, and fry the onions until they begin to soften.

4 Add the mince to the pan and fry until it is no longer pink.

5 Add the garlic, mushrooms, chilli, passata, water and stock, bring to the boil and then simmer for 5 minutes. Season well with salt and pepper.

6 Add the olives, spinach and pasta to the pan and mix together. Pour into the casserole dish.

7 Sprinkle the breadcrumbs over the top and then distribute the mozzarella over the top.

8 Place in the oven for 15–20 minutes or until the top is nicely browned.

Get out all the ingredients before you start; it makes cooking a lot calmer.

Mustard Chicken & Pancetta Gratin

Quick and easy to make. You could exchange the pancetta for 8 rashers of chopped up, streaky bacon if you like.

5 medium **potatoes**, cut into ½cm slices

2 tablespoons **olive oil**

1 **onion**, sliced

200g **pancetta lardons**

250g **mushrooms**, sliced

3 **chicken breasts**, cut into bite-size pieces

1 mug/300ml **single cream**

2 tablespoons **thyme leaves**

1 tablespoon **wholegrain mustard**

½ mug grated **Parmesan**

1 Add the potatoes to a pan of boiling water and simmer for 5 minutes until tender. Remove from the pan and set to one side until needed.

2 Heat the oil in a large frying pan, or wok, and fry the onion and pancetta until it begins to brown.

3 Add the mushrooms and chicken and fry until the chicken is cooked through. Season well with salt and pepper.

4 Pour into a large casserole dish and arrange the cooked potatoes over the top.

5 Preheat the grill.

6 Mix together the cream, thyme leaves and wholegrain mustard. Pour over the potatoes and sprinkle the Parmesan over the top.

7 Place under the grill for 5-8 minutes, or until the cheese has begun to brown.

Florentine Chicken Bake

Florentine dishes tend to have lots of spinach in them and are often topped with mozzarella, so this bake fits the brief nicely.

Gluten-free: use gluten-free pasta and stock cube and gluten-free plain flour in the sauce.

---

3 mugs **pasta**

1 tablespoon **olive oil**

3 **chicken breasts**, cut into bite-sized pieces

2 tablespoons **plain flour**

1 mug **water**

1 **chicken stock cube**

2 tablespoons **sun-dried tomato purée**

100g **Philadelphia cream cheese**

250g **fresh spinach**, roughly chopped

250g **mozzarella** cheese

½ mug grated **Parmesan**

1 Preheat the grill.

2 Put the pasta on to cook. Once cooked, drain and return to the pan.

3 Meanwhile, heat the oil in a large saucepan or wok. Add the chicken breast and fry until no longer pink.

4 Add the flour and mix. Add the water, stock cube and tomato purée and bring to the boil, stirring frequently. Add the Philadelphia and stir on a low heat until it melts.

5 Add the spinach and cook until it wilts; about 1 minute. Add the cooked pasta and mix together.

6 Pour into a casserole dish. Arrange the mozzarella over the top and then sprinkle over the Parmesan. Place under the grill for about 5 minutes, or until the cheese bubbles and browns.

Chicken, Pancetta & Leek Bake

Gluten-free: use gluten-free flour, pasta and bread.

Sauce

50g **butter**, measure using packet

2 tablespoons **plain flour**

2 mugs **milk**

1 teaspoon **mustard**

1 mug grated **Cheddar cheese**

2 mugs **pasta**

1 tablespoon **olive oil**

125g pack **pancetta lardons**

3 medium **leeks**, sliced

2 large **chicken breasts**, cut into bite-sized pieces

Topping

2 slices **crusty white bread**, made into breadcrumbs

2 tablespoons freshly chopped **basil**

1/2 mug grated **Parmesan cheese**

salt and **pepper**

1 Make the sauce by melting the butter in a saucepan, add the flour and mix to a paste. Allow to bubble for 30 seconds, before adding the milk, mustard and cheese. Mix it together, bring to the boil and stir with a small whisk to prevent lumps forming. Leave to one side until needed.

2 Cook the pasta. Once cooked, drain and return to the pan.

3 Meanwhile, preheat the grill.

4 Heat the oil in a large saucepan or wok. Add the pancetta and cook until it begins to brown.

5 Add the leeks and cook until they begin to soften.

6 Add the chicken and cook for 2-3 minutes until cooked through.

7 Add the sauce and the pasta. Mix together and pour into a large casserole dish.

8 Mix the topping ingredients and sprinkle over the top. Place under the grill for about 5 minutes until browned.

Leek & Salmon Pie

Gluten-free: use gluten-free, plain flour in the sauce.

5 medium **potatoes**, cut into 2cm dice (no need to peel)

75g **butter**, measure using packet

2 medium **leeks**, sliced

2 tablespoons **plain flour**

1 1/2 mugs /450ml **milk**

300ml **cream**, double or single

4 **salmon steaks**, cut into bite-sized pieces

1 mug frozen **peas**, defrosted

2 tablespoons freshly chopped **dill**

1/2 mug **Parmesan**

1 Preheat the oven to 180°C fan oven/200°C/ gas 6. Grease a large casserole dish.

2 Put the potatoes on to boil and simmer for 10 minutes. Drain and return to the pan. Add 25g of the butter and shake the pan around to distribute.

3 Add another 25g of the butter to a large frying pan and fry the leeks until they begin to soften and brown. Put the leeks in the casserole dish, along with the defrosted peas.

4 Add the last 25g butter to the frying pan, along with the flour, and cook on a medium heat until the flour is absorbed. Add the milk and cream to the pan and gently bring to the boil, stirring all the time. Add the fish, peas and dill to the sauce and cook, on a medium heat, for 2 minutes. The fish does not need to be cooked through, as it will go in the oven.

5 Pour the sauce and the fish into the casserole dish and mix with the leeks. Pile the potatoes on top and sprinkle the grated Parmesan over.

6 Place in the oven for 20 minutes. The top should be lightly browned.

Chorizo Boulangerie

Super-quick to prepare, but needs a bit longer in the oven. This makes for an ideal mid-week dish when you get in from work and want to quickly throw something in the oven and then relax while it cooks.

Gluten-free: make sure the chorizo and stock pot are gluten-free.

5 medium **potatoes**, unpeeled and cut into 2cm slices

1 **onion**, sliced

250g **chestnut mushrooms**, sliced

200g chopped **chorizo**

1/2 mug **hot water**

1 **veg stock pot**

1/2 mug grated **Parmesan**

1 Preheat the oven to 180°C fan oven/200°C/gas 6. Grease a medium casserole dish.

2 Place the potatoes, onions, mushrooms and chorizo in layers in the casserole dish.

3 Dissolve the stock pot in the water and pour over.

4 Sprinkle the grated Parmesan over the top and place in the oven for 45-50 minutes, until nicely browned.

£1.76 /PERSON · SERVES 4 · EASE ★★★☆☆ · PREP 25 MINS · COOK 30 MINS · OK TO FREEZE · GF OPTION

Cider Pork & Bacon Pie
with Cauliflower & Potato Mash

This is a good, everyday pie, using pork mince, which is slightly less expensive than lamb or beef. Do not be tempted to get the really cheap pork mince, as it tends to be full of fat.

Gluten-free: use gluten-free plain flour in the sauce.

5 medium **potatoes**, peeled and cut into 2cm chunks

1 small **cauliflower**, cut into small pieces

3/4 mug grated **Cheddar cheese**

1 teaspoon **wholegrain mustard**

Filling

150g **streaky bacon**

1 **onion**, sliced

500g **pork mince**

2 **leeks**, sliced

1 tablespoon **plain flour**

1 mug/300ml **cider**

1 **veg stock cube**

1 Preheat the oven to 200°C fan oven/220°C/ gas 7. Grease a large casserole dish.

2 Put the potatoes and the cauliflower in a saucepan of boiling water. Bring to the boil and then turn down to simmer for 10 minutes. Drain and return to the pan. Add the cheese and mustard and mash together.

3 Meanwhile, fry the bacon in a large frying pan until it is crispy. Remove from the pan, cut into smaller pieces and set to one side until needed.

4 In the same frying pan, fry the onions until they become soft. Add the mince and fry until it is no longer pink.

5 Add the leeks and fry for 2 minutes.

6 Add the flour and stir well.

7 Add the cider and the stock cubes. Mix together, bring to the boil and season. Add the chopped bacon and pour into the casserole dish.

8 Put the mash on top. Place in the oven for 25-30 minutes, or until the top is browned.

Tagliatelle Tuna Bake
with Mushroom & Broccoli

Tuna bake is always a great, economic way to feed the family. This one is so tasty, looks good and also has some healthy veg incorporated.

Gluten-free: use gluten-free pasta.

---

6 nests of **tagliatelle**

1 small head of **broccoli**, cut into florets

1 tablespoon **olive oil**

250g **mushrooms**, sliced

1 bunch **spring onions**, sliced

1 mug defrosted **frozen peas**

200g **Philadelphia cheese with garlic and herbs**

100g **crème fraîche**

2 x 185g tins **tuna**, drained and flaked

1 mug grated **Parmesan** cheese

1 Put the tagliatelle and broccoli into a large saucepan of boiling water. Bring to the boil and then turn down to simmer for 5 minutes. Drain and return to the pan.

2 Heat the oil in a wok and fry the mushrooms and spring onions for 1 minute.

3 Add the peas, Philadelphia and crème fraîche. Heat through gently and season well. Add the tuna and gently mix.

4 Add the drained pasta and broccoli and mix together.

5 Pour into a large casserole dish. Sprinkle the cheese over the top and place under a hot grill for 5 minutes or until the cheese begins to brown.

FRIENDS AROUND

When you have friends over, you want to make something a little special, but not be stuck in the kitchen all night while everyone else has fun. Here are some ideas that fit the bill. Some you can prepare beforehand, like 'Mango Chicken Salad'. Others, like 'Paprika Salmon', are really quick to finish off once your friends arrive.

Beef Steak Salad

2 tablespoons **mustard powder**

1 teaspoon freshly ground **black pepper**

3 **rump steaks**

1 tablespoon **olive oil**

2 tablespoons **honey**

Salad

2 **little gem lettuces**, sliced

200g **radishes**, thinly sliced

2 large **carrots**, cut into thin strips, using a peeler

2 tablespoons **pine nuts**

Dressing

2 tablepoons **olive oil**

juice of a **lemon**

1 teaspoon **sugar**

salt and **pepper**

1 tablespoon freshly chopped **basil**

1 tablespoon freshly chopped **parsley**

1 large **ciabatta**, cut in half horizontally

1 clove **garlic**, peeled, but not chopped

1   Put the mustard and pepper on a large plate and season with salt. Press the steaks into the mixture and rub it onto the meat. Leave to stand for 5 minutes.

2   Meanwhile, prepare the salad ingredients and mix together the dressing ingredients.

3   Grill the ciabatta. Once lightly browned, remove from the grill and rub the garlic lightly over the surface. Cut into chunks.

4   Heat the oil in a frying pan and fry the steaks, for 2 minutes each side, on a high heat. If you like well done steak, turn down the heat and fry for another 2 minutes each side. Remove from the heat and drizzle over the honey. Turn over in the pan to coat both sides with the honey. Remove from the pan and cut into thin strips.

5   Arrange the meal on a sharing platter, or board. Pour over the dressing and any excess juices from the pan or chopping board.

Thai Pork Curry

Gluten-free: make sure the curry sauce and fish sauce are gluten-free.

1 tablespoon **toasted sesame oil**

3 **pork steaks**, cut into thin strips

6 **spring onions**, sliced

1 **red pepper**, cut into 2cm chunks

125g **mushrooms**, sliced

400ml **thick and creamy coconut milk**

2 tablespoons **Thai red curry paste**

1 tablespoon **fish sauce**

can **bamboo shoots**, drained

1 teaspoon **brown sugar**

2 tablespoons freshly chopped **coriander**

2 x 300g packs **fresh rice noodles**

1 Heat the oil in a wok, or large frying pan. Add the pork and fry on a high heat for 2–3 minutes, or until it begins to brown. Remove from the pan. Set to one side until needed.

2 Add the onions, peppers and mushrooms to the pan and fry for 2–3 minutes, or until the peppers begin to brown.

3 Add the coconut milk, curry paste and fish sauce to the pan and bring to the boil.

4 Add the bamboo shoots, sugar and coriander to the pan, along with the pork, and simmer for 1 minute.

5 Put the rice noodles in a bowl and pour boiling water over them. Leave to stand for 1 minute and then drain. Serve with the curry.

Cook foolproof rice in 15 minutes. Put 2 mugs boiling water in a pan, add 1 mug basmati rice. Bring to the boil. Simmer with a lid on the pan for 12 minutes. The water should be absorbed and the rice fluffy.

Trout Fillets with Beetroot Salad

Beetroot is not your 'run-of-the-mill' ingredient, so this, along with the thinly sliced radish, makes for an excellent summer salad, with a difference.

Almond Sauce

2 tablespoons **soured cream**

2 tablespoons freshly chopped **basil**

1 tablespoon **olive oil**

2 tablespoons **toasted, flaked almonds**, finely chopped

salt and **pepper**

Dressing

2 tablespoons **olive oil**

juice of a **lemon**

1/2 teaspoon **sugar**

salt and **pepper**

1 tablespoon **olive oil**

400g **trout fillets**

1 bag **rocket salad**

3 **gherkins**, sliced

100g **radishes**, finely sliced

4 **cooked beetroot**, cut into sticks

1 Mix together the almond sauce ingredients and set to one side until needed.

2 Mix together the dressing ingredients.

3 Heat the tablespoon of olive oil in the frying pan and add the trout fillets; they will take only 2–3 minutes to cook through. Remove from the pan and take the skins off. Flake the fish gently.

4 Arrange the salad on the plates. Drizzle over the dressing and serve with the almond cream.

🌐 We have got a beautiful goats' cheese salad online:
www.noshbooks.com/goats-cheese

Lamb Chops with Pancetta Salad & Yoghurt Dressing

Gluten-free: use gluten-free bread for the salad.

Dressing

juice of a **lemon**

1/2 mug **Parmesan cheese**

4 tablespoons **Greek yoghurt**

2 tablespoons **fresh mint**, chopped

2 tablespoons **olive oil**

salt and **pepper**

Salad

1 tablespoon **olive oil**

2 slices **wholemeal bread**

100g sliced **pancetta** (you can use streaky bacon)

125g **cherry tomatoes**, halved

3 **roasted red peppers** (from a jar), roughly chopped

1/2 x 100g bag **salad**

8 **small lamb chops**

1 Mix the dressing ingredients together.

2 To make the croutons, heat the oil in a frying pan and fry the bread until it is brown on both sides. Take out of the pan and cut into small squares.

3 Fry the pancetta lightly; don't make it too crisp. Remove from the pan and cut into bite-sized pieces.

4 Mix all the salad ingredients together.

5 Heat a little oil in a frying pan and fry the lamb chops for 2 minutes each side. If you have larger, or thicker, chops, you will need to fry for a little longer. Season well.

6 Serve everything together.

Mango Chicken Salad

Super quick and easy recipe. The curry paste is not too spicy for children to try. If they are all grown up, then you can add more spice to taste, but not too much, or you will drown the other more subtle flavours.

Gluten-free: make sure the curry paste is gluten-free.

3 **chicken breasts**, cut into strips

1 dessertspoon of **mild curry paste**

juice of a **lemon**

1 tablespoon **olive oil**

Dressing

150ml **natural yoghurt**

1 dessertspoon **mango chutney**

100g **watercress**

1/2 **cucumber**, cut into thin strips

6 **spring onions**, sliced

1 medium **cos lettuce**, sliced

1 ripe **mango**, peeled and cut into slices

1 Put the chicken breast pieces in a bowl and add the curry paste and lemon juice. Mix together and leave for 10 minutes.

2 Meanwhile, mix together the dressing ingredients and set aside until needed.

3 Prepare the salad ingredients and divide between the plates.

4 Heat the oil in a large frying pan and fry the chicken pieces on a medium heat, taking care not to burn the curry paste. They should take no longer than 5 minutes to cook through. Check one of the thickest pieces to make sure.

5 Serve on the salad with the dressing drizzled over.

🌐 Like sweet chicken dishes? Here's another one:
www.noshbooks.com/sweetnsour

£1.63 /PERSON · SERVES 4 · EASE ★★★★★ · PREP 20 MINS · COOK 15 MINS · GF OPTION

Koftas from Kashmir

Gluten-free: use gluten-free plain flour in the koftas.

Spice mix

2 teaspoons **ground cumin**

2 teaspoons **ground coriander**

2 teaspoons **garam masala**

1/2 teaspoon **hot chilli powder**

1/2 teaspoon **ground turmeric**

Koftas

500g **minced lamb**

4 cloves **garlic**, finely chopped

12 **dried apricots**, chopped finely

2 tablespoons grated fresh **ginger** (a pile the size of a table tennis ball!)

2 tablespoons **natural yoghurt**

2 tablespoons **plain flour**

25g **butter**, measure using packet

1 large **onion**, chopped

2 tablespoons **milk powder**

3 tablespoons **ground almonds**

2 teaspoons **sugar**

2 mugs **hot water**

rice and **fresh coriander** to serve

1 Combine the spice mix in a small bowl.

2 In a large bowl, mix together the kofta ingredients, along with half of the spice mix. Roll the mixture into around 20 small balls with your hands (they will expand a little during the cooking process). Dust over with the flour.

3 Heat the butter in a large pan and add the onion. Once browned, turn down the heat and add the rest of the spice mixture. Stir for about 30 seconds until the aroma is wonderful!

4 Add the remaining ingredients (excluding the rice and coriander) and bring to the boil.

5 Add the koftas to the pan, bring back to the boil and turn down to simmer gently, with a lid on, for 10 minutes. After 5 minutes, check and gently turn the koftas.

6 Put the rice on to cook. Once cooked, leave with a lid on to keep warm until ready to serve.

7 Remove the lid from the koftas and simmer for 5 minutes until the sauce thickens. Take off the heat and leave to cool slightly. Serve with rice.

£ 1.37 /PERSON | SERVES 4 | EASE ★★★★☆ | PREP 25 MINS | COOK 40 MINS | GF OPTION

Southern Fried Chicken with Polenta Chips

Gluten-free: use gluten-free, plain flour in the coating for the chicken.

---

ready-made polenta

2 tablespoons **olive oil**

Sauce

2 tablespoons **mayo**

2 tablespoons **yoghurt**

juice of a **lemon**

1 tablespoon **honey**

4 teaspoons **dried oregano**

2 teaspoons **paprika**

1 teaspoon **chilli powder**

2 teaspoons **dried mustard**

1/2 mug/100g **plain flour**

2 tablespoons **honey**

juice of a **lemon**

3 **chicken breasts**, cut into strips

1 Preheat the oven, 200°C fan oven/220°C/gas 7.

2 Cut the polenta into chips. Put on two baking trays, drizzle with oil and season with salt and pepper. Carefully mix together to make sure everything is coated. Place in the oven for 30–40 minutes.

3 Mix together the sauce ingredients and set to one side until needed.

4 Put the oregano, paprika, chilli powder, mustard, flour and salt and pepper in a bowl. Put the honey and lemon in another bowl. Mix the honey and lemon together in a bowl. Dip the chicken pieces, first in the honey mix, and then in the spice mix. Try to attach as much as possible to the chicken.

5 Heat the oil in a large frying pan and fry the chicken for 2–3 minutes each side. The outside should be nicely browned and the inside cooked through.

6 Serve with the polenta chips and the sauce.

Chilli Cashew Chicken with Hoisin Sauce & Bamboo Shoots

Really simple, tasty dish, which most older children should love. Much less expensive that a Chinese takeaway. The longer you simmer the chilli, the hotter the dish will be.

Gluten-free: make sure the hoisin and stock cube are gluten-free.

---

1 ¹/2 mugs, **basmati rice**

2 mugs **water** + 1 **chicken stock cube**

2 **carrots**, cut into thin sticks

250g tin **bamboo shoots**

3 medium **chicken breasts**, cut into thin strips

¹/2 x 290g jar **hoisin sauce**

3 teaspoons **cornflour** mixed into 2 tablespoons **water**

³/4 mug/125g **cashews**

6 **spring onions**, sliced

1 **fat red chilli**, chopped (optional)

1　Put the rice in 3 mugs of boiling water and bring to the boil. Simmer for 12 minutes with a lid on the pan.

2　Heat the water and the chicken stock in a wok, add the carrots and simmer for 5 minutes.

3　Add the bamboo shoots and simmer for 3 minutes.

4　Add the chicken and simmer until the meat is no longer pink. Check the thickest piece.

5　Add the rest of the ingredients, bring to the boil and simmer for one minute.

6　Serve with the rice.

Soy Salmon with Wasabi Mash & Pak Choi

The wasabi mash is almost a Far Eastern version of Mustard Mash, but the wasabi is a lot hotter. The wasabi paste will keep for a while in the fridge, so will be there when you are almost certain to repeat this meal

Gluten-free: make sure the soy sauce is gluten-free.

Marinade

4 tablespoons **soy sauce**

2 tablespoons **toasted sesame oil**

3 tablespoons **maple syrup**

juice of 2 **limes**

4 **salmon** fillets

Mash

4 medium **potatoes**, peeled and cut into 2cm chunks

1/4 mug **double cream**

4 **spring onions**, chopped

1 teaspoon **wasabi paste**

4 **pak choi**, sliced

1 tablespoon **toasted sesame seeds**

1 Mix together the marinade ingredients and add the salmon.

2 Cover and leave for 30 minutes.

3 Once the salmon has marinaded, simmer the potatoes in salted water for 10 minutes. Drain and return to the pan. Add the rest of the mash ingredients and mash together. Put a lid on the pan and set to one side until needed.

4 On medium heat, put a tablespoon of sesame oil in a frying pan. Remove the salmon from the marinade (keep the marinade for later) and fry the salmon until cooked through. Should take about 5 minutes, depending on the thickness of the fish.

5 Take the fish out of the pan, add the marinade to the pan, simmer for 1 minute and then remove from the heat.

6 In a large frying pan, or wok, heat another tablespoon of sesame oil. Add the pak choi and fry for 30 seconds. Add 1 tablespoon water, put a lid on the pan, and cook for a further 1 minute. Season.

7 Serve the salmon on top of the mash, with the pak choi to one side. Pour the sauce over. Sprinkle over with sesame seeds.

Seared Tuna with Anchovy Dressing

You can watch the tuna cooking as the sides turn from pink to white. Do not allow it to cook right through. Tuna will continue to cook even when taken out of the pan. If you cook it too much, it will go dry. Leave it a little rare in the middle (see photo).

Gluten-free: use gluten-free bread for the breadcrumbs.

Dressing

4 **anchovies**, finely chopped

juice of a **lemon**

3 tablespoons **mayo**

2 tablespoons **olive oil**

Salad

2 **little gem lettuces**, chopped

1/2 **cucumber**, cut into sticks

4 **spring onions**, sliced lengthways

2 slices **wholemeal bread**, made into breadcrumbs

zest of a **lemon**

2 tablespoons freshly chopped **basil**

4 fresh **tuna steaks**

2 tablespoons **olive oil**

1 Mix together the dressing ingredients and season. Prepare the salad.

2 Mix together the breadcrumbs, lemon zest, basil and then season. Put on a plate and press the tuna steaks into the mixture.

3 Heat the oil in a large frying pan and fry the tuna steaks until each side is browned, but still rare in the centre.

4 Cut each steak into 3 or 4 and serve on top of the salad. Drizzle over the dressing.

£ 1.82 /PERSON   SERVES 4   EASE ★★☆☆☆   PREP 30 MINS   GF OPTION

Pork Tacos with a Haricot Bean Salsa

Gluten-free: make sure the tacos are gluten-free.

Bean Salsa

1 tablespoon **olive oil**

6 **tomatoes**, chopped

2 cloves **garlic**, finely chopped

400g tin **haricot beans**

2 tablespoons freshly chopped **basil**

2 tablespoons **tomato purée**

1/2 mug **water**

1 **fat red chilli**, finely chopped

4 **pork steaks**

1 tablespoon **paprika**

1 tablespoon **ground coriander**

1 tablespoon **olive oil**

2 **little gem lettuces**

8 **taco shells**

Dressing

4 tablespoons **natural yoghurt**

juice of 1/2 **lemon**

2 tablespoons freshly chopped **coriander**

1 Heat the oil in a medium-sized saucepan. Add the tomatoes and garlic and fry for 2 minutes. Add the rest of the salsa ingredients, apart from the basil, and bring to the boil. Simmer for 2 minutes. Add the basil and set to one side until needed.

2 Put the paprika, ground coriander and some salt and pepper on a large plate. Press the pork steaks into the spice mixture. Rub the spices in.

3 Preheat the oven to 180°C fan oven/200°C/ gas 6. Put the tacos on a baking sheet and heat in the oven for 2 minutes.

4 Heat the oil in a large frying pan and add the steaks. Fry for 2 minutes each side. If the steaks are thicker, fry for 1 minute longer each side. The outsides should be dark and crunchy and the insides must be cooked through. Check the thickest. Remove from the pan and slice into thin strips.

5 Mix together the dressing ingredients.

6 Arrange the ingredients in the taco shells and enjoy. Be warned, you will get messy eating them!

Beijing-Style Crispy Chicken Pancakes

If you want to make curly spring onions, place them, thinly sliced, in a bowl of ice cold water. Leave them for about 5 minutes and they will curl. These Chinese pancakes may be tricky to get a hold of in all supermarkets. If your local one does not stock them, have a look around to see if there is a Chinese supermarket near you.

3 **chicken breasts**

4 tablespoons **hoisin sauce**

1 tablespoon **olive oil**

12 **Chinese pancakes**

1/2 **cucumber**, cut into sticks

12 **spring onions**, thinly sliced, lengthways

4 tablespoons **hoisin sauce** + 1 tablespoon **water**

1 Put the chicken breasts between sheets of cling film and give them a 'bit of a bash' with a rolling pin to flatten them. Pour over the 4 tablespoons of hoisin and spread it over the chicken.

2 Heat the oil in a large frying pan and fry the chicken breasts for 2 minutes each side; the outsides should be browned and crispy. Check that they are cooked through.

3 Take out of the pan and cut into thin strips.

4 Heat the pancakes as per instructions on the packet.

5 Serve the slices of chicken with the pancakes, cucumber, onions and hoisin sauce.

£2.79 /PERSON

SERVES 4

EASE ★★☆☆☆

PREP 25 MINS

GF OPTION

Paprika Salmon with Soy & Honey

I love salmon as it is such a versatile fish. You can make it into pies, or dress it up in so many ways; it still retains its flavour. Here we have spiced it up and set it alongside some crunchy pak choi.

Gluten-free: make sure soy sauce is gluten-free.

1 mug **basmati rice**

2 mugs **boiling water**

1 teaspoon **pilau rice seasoning**

2 **pak choi**

1 tablespoon **paprika**

4 **salmon steaks**

1 tablespoon **toasted sesame oil**

2 tablespoons **soy sauce**

2 tablespoons **runny honey**

1 Put the rice and pilau rice seasoning on to cook in a large saucepan. After about 10 minutes, add the chopped pak choi and return the lid to the pan. Leave for 2 minutes. Mix together, leaving the lid on the pan, and set aside until needed.

2 Put the paprika on a plate and press the salmon steaks into it.

3 Heat the oil in a frying pan and fry the salmon, taking care not to burn the paprika. Once the salmon is cooked through, add the soy and honey to the pan and allow to simmer for 1 minute.

4 Serve the flaked fish on top of the rice and drizzle over the sauce.

Chicken in Black Bean Sauce

Gluten-free: make sure the stock cube, soy and black bean sauce are gluten-free.

1 1/2 mugs **basmati rice**

1 tablespoon **olive oil**

3 **chicken breasts**, cut into small pieces

1 bunch **spring onions**, chopped

6 **mushrooms**, sliced

1 **fat red chilli**, chopped

1/2 mug **water** + 1 **chicken stock cube**, crumbled

1 teaspoon **cornflour**

1 tablespoon **dark soy sauce**

1/2 x 195g bottle **black bean sauce**

1 Put the rice on to cook. Once cooked, leave the lid on the pan and set to one side until needed.

2 Heat the oil in a large frying pan, or wok. Add the chicken and fry until it is no longer pink.

3 Add the spring onions, mushrooms and chilli and fry for 1 minute.

4 Mix together the water, stock cube, cornflour, soy and black bean sauce. Add to the pan and bring to the boil. The sauce should thicken.

5 Serve with the rice.

Cook foolproof rice in 15 minutes. Put 2 mugs boiling water in a pan, add 1 mug basmati rice. Bring to the boil. Simmer with a lid on the pan for 12 minutes. The water should be absorbed and the rice fluffy.

Pan Roasted Marsala Chicken with Parsnip Mash

This is a bit of a special meal for two. The sauce is delicious. Marsala will keep in the bottle for ages, a bit like sherry, so don't worry about only using a small amount from the bottle you buy, as you can use the rest another time.

Gluten-free: use gluten-free plain flour in the gravy.

2 medium **potatoes**, peeled and cut into chunks

2 medium **parsnips**, peeled and cut into chunks

25g **butter**, measure using packet

1 tablespoon **olive oil**

2 **chicken breasts**

125g **chestnut mushrooms**, sliced

1/2 mug/150ml **Marsala wine**

1 teaspoon **plain flour**

10g softened **butter**, measure using packet

green beans to serve

1 Put the potatoes and the parsnips in a pan of boiling water and bring to the boil. Turn down to simmer for 10-12 minutes, or until the veg is tender. Drain and return to the pan. Add the 25g butter, season well with salt and pepper, and mash. Put a lid on the pan and set to one side.

2 Meanwhile heat the oil in a frying pan. Add the chicken breasts and season well with salt and pepper. Fry on each side for 2 minutes on a high heat. Turn down the heat and fry, with a lid on the pan, for 3-4 minutes on each side (depending on the thickness of the chicken).

3 Remove the chicken from the pan and add the mushrooms. Fry for 1 minute and then add the Marsala. Simmer for 2-3 minutes.

4 Mix together the flour and softened butter, add to the pan and stir into the sauce. Simmer until it thickens slightly.

5 Serve with the mash, chicken breast and beans.

Pan-Fried Chicken with Lime & Coconut Sauce

1 ½ mugs **basmati rice**

1 teaspoon **pillau rice seasoning**

2 tablespoons freshly chopped **coriander**

1 tablespoon **toasted sesame oil**

3 **chicken breasts**

Lime and coconut sauce

1 tablespoon **toasted sesame oil**

1 clove **garlic**

2 tablespoons freshly grated **ginger**

juice of a **lime**

1 **chicken stock cube**

2 teaspoons **fish sauce**

1 teaspoon **sugar**

400ml can **coconut milk**

1 tablespoon **toasted sesame oil**

4 **pak choi**, sliced

1   Put the rice on to cook in 3 mugs of boiling water. Add the pilau rice seasoning and simmer for 12 minutes. Just before you serve the rice, add the chopped coriander.

2   Heat the oil in a frying pan and add the chicken breasts. Season well. Cook on a fairly high heat for 2 minutes each side. Turn the heat down to medium and cook for a further 4 minutes each side, with a lid on the pan. If the chicken breasts are really small, then cook for less time. Remove from the pan and set to one side until needed.

3   To make the sauce, heat the toasted sesame oil in a small saucepan and gently fry the garlic and ginger. Add the rest of the sauce ingredients and simmer gently for 5–6 minutes.

4   Heat the other tablespoon of toasted sesame oil in the frying pan and stir-fry the pak choi for 1 minute or until it begins to wilt slightly; it needs to be quite 'al dente'.

🌍 Have you ever tried puy lentils? Why not try this recipe: www.noshbooks.com/spiced-chicken

Pan-Fried Salmon on Prawn Rice Salad with Marie Rose Sauce

Marie Rose Sauce

4 tablespoons **mayo**

1 tablespoon **tomato purée**

6 **green olives**, chopped

1 **ready-roasted pepper**, chopped

2 tablespoons **wine vinegar**

1 teaspoon **sugar**

salt and **pepper**

Rice salad

1 mug **basmati rice**

1/3 **cucumber**, diced

4 **pickled gherkins**, chopped

200g **prawns**

juice of a **lemon**

1 tablespoon **olive oil**

1 tablespoon **olive oil**

4 small **salmon steaks**

bag of **salad leaves**

1 Mix together the sauce ingredients.

2 Cook the rice in 2 mugs of boiling water. Once cooked, turn out onto a plate to cool slightly.

3 Prepare the rest of the rice salad ingredients and place in a mixing bowl. Add the cooled rice and mix.

4 Heat the oil in a frying pan and fry the salmon for 2–3 minutes each side, depending on the thickness of the steaks. Season with salt and pepper.

5 Arrange the salad leaves on the plates, pile in the rice salad and place the salmon steaks over the top. Drizzle over the dressing.

Do you want another idea for using salmon? Go to: www.noshbooks.com/posh-salmon

£ 1.33 /PERSON   SERVES 4   EASE ★★★☆☆   PREP 25 MINS   GF

Peppered Pork with Apple & Blue Cheese Salad

Pork and apples are always a great duo and the addition of the blue cheese is a lovely complement to the more familiar combination.

Dressing

75g **blue cheese**

2 tablespoons **olive oil**

4 tablespoons **Greek yoghurt**

juice of a **lemon**

salt and **pepper**

1 tablespoon freshly ground **black pepper**

4 lean **pork steaks**

salt

1 tablespoon **olive oil**

Salad

1 bag **rocket leaves**

1/2 **cucumber**, cut into sticks

4 **spring onions**. cut into thin strips

2 **Golden Delicious apples**, cut into thin sticks

1 Mix together the dressing ingredients and blend with a hand-held blender, if you have one, otherwise, squash the cheese with a fork. It doesn't matter if the dressing is a bit chunky.

2 Put the ground pepper on a plate and press the pork steaks into it to evenly coat them. Season with the salt. Heat the oil in a frying pan and fry the pork steaks for about 2 minutes each side, or more if they are thicker steaks. Remove from the pan and set to one side until needed.

3 Meanwhile, mix the salad ingredients together in a bowl. Divide between the plates and drizzle over the dressing. Cut the pork into strips and place on the top and serve.

1.12 /PERSON SERVES 4 EASE ★★★☆☆ PREP 30 MINS GF OPTION

Sweet & Sour Spicy Cod

Gluten-free: make sure the soy sauce is gluten-free.

Mash

4 medium **potatoes**, cubed, no need to peel

1 small **broccoli**, cut into florets

2 mugs **frozen peas**, defrosted

1 tablespoon freshly chopped **mint**

50g **butter**, measure using packet

2 tablespoons **olive oil**

4 **cod steaks**

Sauce

2 cloves **garlic**, finely chopped

1 **fat red chilli**, cut into rings

3 tablespoons **red wine vinegar**

1 tablespoon **soft brown sugar**

4 tablespoons **soy sauce**

4 tablespoons **water** + 1 teaspoon **cornflour**

1 Put the potatoes on to boil, simmer for 5 minutes and then add the broccoli. After a further five minutes, add the defrosted peas and simmer for 2 minutes. Drain and return to the pan. Add the mint and the butter and mash slightly, leave things a bit chunky. Set to one side until needed.

2 Heat the oil in a large frying pan and add the cod. Fry on a medium heat until lightly browned on each side and cooked through. Remove from the pan and set to one side.

3 Add the garlic and chillies to the pan and fry for 30 seconds.

4 In a mug, mix the red wine vinegar, sugar, soy, water and cornflour together. Add to the pan and stir well; the sauce should thicken.

5 Serve the fish on top of the mash and pour the sauce over.

Prawn Jambalaya

Jambalaya originates in the Caribbean, but has strong Spanish influence, quite like a paella. It usually is a mix of chicken, sausage, fish, vegetables and rice. We have missed out the chicken here!

Gluten-free: make sure the chorizo and stock cube are gluten-free.

1 1/2 mugs **rice**

1 tablespoon **olive oil**

1 **onion**, chopped

1 clove **garlic**, chopped

1/2 **green pepper**, chopped

100g diced **chorizo**

1 teaspoon **chilli powder**

1 teaspoon **turmeric**

6 **tomatoes**, chopped

1/2 mug/150ml **water** + 1 **chicken stock cube**

350g **cooked prawns**

1 tablespoon freshly chopped **coriander**

1 Cook the rice and leave in the pan, with the lid on, until needed.

2 Heat the oil in a wok or large frying pan. Add the onion, garlic and pepper and cook until they begin to soften. Add the chorizo and fry until it begins to brown.

3 Add the chilli powder, turmeric, tomatoes, water and stock cube and bring to the boil. Simmer for 2 minutes.

4 Add the prawns and coriander and cook for 1 minute.

5 Stir in the cooked rice and serve.

CAKES &
DESSERTS

Love cakes and cookies, but don't want complicated and lengthy prep? I have included some that only take 25 minutes from start to finish. When Ben is craving chocolate, he sometimes challenges me to see how quickly I can make him some chocolate cookies. My fastest, so far, has been 22 minutes, but that is with a bit of practice! The 'Brioche Pudding' takes only 5-10 minutes to prepare and is delicious.

Orange & Ginger Cookies with Pecans

You can actually leave this dough for a couple of days in the fridge and cook fresh cookies whenever you want them. These cookies never last long in our house and, considering that they don't have any chocolate in them, it is quite a recommendation!

175g softened **butter**, measure using packet

3/4 mug/175g **granulated sugar**

1 **egg**

rind of an **orange**

1 tablespoon juice from **orange**

2 mugs/360g **self-raising flour**

1/2 mug/50g **pecan nuts**, chopped

4 pieces of **crystallised ginger**, chopped

1 Beat the butter and sugar together in a mixing bowl until it is light and fluffy.

2 Add the egg, orange rind and orange juice and beat until smooth.

3 Add the flour, pecans and ginger and mix to a dough.

4 Turn out onto a floured surface and divide into 2. Roll each half into a 'sausage' about 4cm in diameter. Wrap in cling film and leave in the fridge for 45 minutes.

5 Preheat the oven to 180°C fan oven/200°C /gas 6. Grease or line a baking tray.

6 The cookie dough will be quite firm by now. Cut with a sharp knife into 1cm thick cookies and place on the baking tray 4cm apart. Bake in the oven for 10 minutes. The cookies will be slightly browned around the edges.

£0.18 /PERSON
 MAKES 18
 EASE ★★★☆☆
 PREP 15 MINS
 COOK 12 MINS
 OK TO FREEZE ❄

Smartie Oat Cookies

You really need a cake tin to store these in, once they are cooked, or they may not last for a day! Ours managed to survive over two days, as our resident, infamous chocoholic, was absent the day they were made.

125g softened **butter**, measure using packet

1 mug/210g **soft brown sugar**

1 teaspoon **vanilla extract**

1 **egg**

1 mug/170g **self-raising flour**

150g pack **Smarties**

1/2 mug **oats**

1 tablespoon **cocoa**

Smarties to decorate

1 Preheat the oven to 180°C fan oven/200°C/gas 6. Grease 2 baking trays.

2 Beat the butter and sugar together. Add the vanilla extract and egg and beat well.

3 Add the flour, Smarties, oats and cocoa. Mix to a stiff dough.

4 Roll into a 30cm 'sausage' and cut into about 24 cookies. Place on the baking trays. Leave space between them, as they spread out. Press a few Smarties in each to decorate.

5 Place in the oven for 12 minutes. The cookies should be crisp on the outside and a little chewy on the inside.

🌐 See another one of our cookie recipes online: www.noshbooks.com/cookie

Almond & White Chocolate Chip Cookies

125g softened **butter**, measure using packet

1 mug/210g **soft brown sugar**

1 **egg**

1 teaspoon **almond extract**

1 1/2 mugs/225g **self-raising flour**

100g packet of **white chocolate chips**

1/2 mug/60g **desiccated coconut**

1/2 mug/60g **toasted flaked almonds**

1 Preheat the oven to 180°C fan oven/200°C/gas 6. Grease 2 baking trays.

2 Beat the butter and sugar together until pale in colour.

3 Add the egg and almond extract and beat until smooth.

4 Add the flour and chocolate chips. Gently mix together to form a soft dough.

5 Divide the mixture into approximately 30 small balls.

6 Put the coconut and almonds on a plate and mix together. Press the dough balls into the coconut and almonds.

7 Place the balls on the baking trays, about 5cm apart, as the dough will spread in the oven.

8 Place in the oven for 14 minutes until the cookies are pale brown. Leave to cool on the trays. The cookies should be crunchy on the outside and a bit chewy on the inside.

Almond & Poppy Seed Cookies

The unusual addition of cream cheese to these cookies ensures that they stay gooey and chewy in the centre.

50g softened **butter**, measure using packet

75g **cream cheese** (Philadelphia)

1 mug/225g **sugar**

1 **egg**

1 teaspoon **vanilla extract**

1 teaspoon **almond extract**

1 1/2 mugs/210g **self-raising flour**

1 tablespoon **poppy seeds**

1/2 mug **flaked almonds**

1 Preheat the oven to 180°C fan oven/200°C/gas 6. Grease 2 baking trays.

2 Beat together the butter, cream cheese and sugar until light and fluffy.

3 Add the egg, vanilla and almond extract and beat well.

4 Add the flour and poppy seeds and mix to a dough.

5 Divide into approximately 30 pieces and roll into balls. Roll them in the flaked almonds. Place on the baking trays and squash each one down a little.

6 Bake in the oven for 12 minutes; the cookies should be slightly browned. They will be slightly chewy in the middle and crisp on the outside.

Chocolate Orange Fudge Fingers

75g **dark chocolate**, broken up

2 tablespoons **cocoa**

1 mug/200g **light brown sugar**

1/3 mug/100ml **hot water**

175g softened **butter**, measure using packet

2 **eggs**

rind of an **orange**

2/3 mug/110g **self-raising flour**

1/2 teaspoon **baking powder**

125ml **soured cream**

100g **chocolate**

1 Preheat the oven to 160°C fan oven/180°C/ gas 4. Grease and line a baking tray.

2 Put the chocolate, cocoa and sugar in a food processor and blend until it resembles crumbs. Add the hot water and whizz for 1 minute. If you do not have a food processor, just grate the chocolate and mix with the sugar, then add the hot water.

3 Add the butter and whizz for 30 seconds. Add the eggs and orange rind and whizz again. Add the flour, baking powder and soured cream and pulse a couple of times.

4 Pour onto the baking tray and put in the oven for 50 minutes. The top should have formed a crust, but the centre will still be a little soggy. Leave to cool.

5 Melt the chocolate in a bowl over simmering water. Drizzle over the cake and allow to set. Cut into whatever shapes you like.

Apricot Goody Bars with Pistachios & Pumpkin Seeds

Good alternative to the expensive 'goody bars' available in the supermarkets. Wrap in greaseproof paper if you want to add them to lunch boxes.

Gluten-free: make sure the oats are gluten-free.

140g **butter**, measure using packet

1 mug/200g **soft light brown sugar**

2 tablespoons **runny honey**

2 mugs/175g **rolled oats**

1/2 mug/75g **pistachio nuts**

1/2 mug/100g **ready-to-eat-dried apricots**, chopped

1 mug/145g **raisins**

1/3 mug/50g **pumpkin seeds**

1 Preheat the oven to 160°C fan oven/180°C/gas 4. Grease and line a 20x30cm traybake tin.

2 Put the butter, sugar and honey in a small pan and heat gently until the butter has melted and the sugar dissolved.

3 In a large bowl, mix the oats, pistachios, apricots, raisins and pumpkin seeds together.

4 Add the contents of the pan and mix together well.

5 Tip into the tin and press down evenly.

6 Place in the oven for 30–35 minutes; the top should be lightly browned.

7 Leave to cool and then cut into small squares.

Chocolate Fudge Cake

This will actually keep in a tin for a few days, but I doubt it will last that long if you have a family like mine! It went down really well in the Nosh kitchen.

2 **eggs**

1/2 mug/150ml **sunflower oil**

1/2 mug/150ml **milk**

397g tin **Carnation Caramel**

1 mug/175g **self-raising flour**

2 1/2 tablespoons **cocoa**

1 teaspoon **bicarb soda**

2/3 mug/150g **caster sugar**

125g **dark chocolate**

1 Preheat the oven to 160°C fan oven/180°C/gas 4. Line 2 x 18cm round cake tins.

2 Whisk together the eggs, oil, milk, and 3 tablespoons of Carnation Caramel until smooth.

3 Mix the flour, cocoa, bicarb and sugar in a large bowl. Add the wet ingredients and mix together gently until smooth.

4 Pour into the 2 tins. It will look as though there is not enough mixture in the tins, but it will rise in the oven. Bake in the oven for 25 minutes.

5 Melt the chocolate in a bowl over a pan of simmering water. Add the rest of the Carnation Caramel and whisk until smooth. Once the cakes have cooled, put 1/3 of the topping in the middle of the cake and the other 2/3 on the top and side.

🌐 Mint and chocolate are a great combo. Agree? Have a look here: www.noshbooks.com/mint-slices

Instant Yoghurt Ice Cream

You don't necessarily need a food processor or hand-held blender for this recipe. Just squish the raspberries with a spoon and add to the yoghurt. You could eat this straight away, but putting it in the freezer firms it up so you can scoop it. Don't leave in the freezer for longer than 90 minutes, as the ice cream becomes quite hard.

500g **frozen raspberries**

600ml **organic full fat yoghurt**

2 tablespoons **runny honey**

Chocolate Sauce

25g **butter**, measure using packet

100g **milk chocolate**

1/2 mug/150ml **double cream**

1 Put the raspberries, yoghurt and honey in a food processor and whiz until the raspberries are completely broken up. Transfer into a dish, or plastic tub, and put in the freezer for 90 minutes.

2 Make the chocolate sauce. Put the ingredients in a small saucepan and gently heat. Allow to bubble for 30 seconds. Set to one side until needed.

3 Serve together.

Strawberry & Almond Pavlovas

This makes lovely, tasty meringues with chewy centres. The almonds and brown sugar give a distinctive flavour. The contrast of the citrus in the juice make for an amazing dessert, which is not too difficult to make.

1 tablespoon **soft dark brown sugar**

3 **egg whites**

3/4 mug/180g **caster sugar**

1/4 mug/35g **toasted, flaked almonds**

juice of an **orange**

1/4 x 454g jar of **blackcurrant jelly jam**

500g **strawberries**

1 mug/300ml **double cream**

1 Preheat the oven to 150°C fan oven/170°C/gas 3. Line 2 baking trays with greaseproof paper.

2 Line another baking tray with greaseproof paper and sprinkle the brown sugar over it. Place under the grill until the sugar melts and begins to bubble. You need to watch the sugar as it will quickly burn. Leave to cool and then crush, with a spoon, or blitz in a processor.

3 Whisk the egg whites in a clean bowl until stiff. Gradually add the caster sugar and beat well until the sugar is dissolved; this should make quite a stiff mixture. Fold in the caramelised sugar and almonds.

4 Spoon tablespoons of the mixture onto the baking sheets; it should make about 8. Place in the oven for 40 minutes. Turn off the oven and leave the meringues in there for another 45 minutes.

5 Put the orange juice and jam in a small pan and gently heat until the jam has dissolved. Chop up the strawberries and add to the pan. Leave to cool.

6 Beat the cream to soft peaks.

7 Serve the meringues with a dollop of cream and the strawberry mixture.

🌐 See other pavlovas online:
www.noshbooks.com/almond-and-pear-pavlova

Brioche Pudding

A truly yummy alternative to plain old bread and butter pudding. This could barely be simpler to make. Slice the bread, pour everything over the top and wack in the oven.

butter to grease the dish

400g **brioche loaf**

250g **frozen** raspberries

4 **eggs**

300ml/1 mug **single cream**

2 tablespoons **caster sugar**

grated rind of a **lemon**

1 teaspoon **vanilla extract**

1 Preheat the oven to 160°C fan oven/180°C/gas 5. Grease a casserole dish with butter.

2 Cut the brioche into 1cm slices and arrange them in the dish. Add the raspberries and tuck them into the bread (see photo).

3 Beat the eggs in a bowl and add the cream, sugar, lemon rind and vanilla. Pour over the brioche as evenly as possible. Leave to stand for 5 minutes, to allow the brioche to absorb the liquid.

4 Place in the oven for 20-25 minutes. The brioche should be lightly browned and the egg mixture set.

Strawberry Muffin 'Millefeuille'

You can make your own muffins, or buy them, but they need to be quite large to make this hold up. Make your own and you will have a few for the next day! Assemble just before serving. You can whip the cream, prepare the strawberries and the chocolate sauce beforehand, so you can construct them at the last minute.

Gluten-free: there is a recipe for gluten-free muffins in our gluten-free book and on our website, www.noshbooks.com.

Muffins
3 mugs/525g **self-raising flour** minus 2 tablespoons

2 tablespoons **cocoa**

1 mug/175g **sugar**

100g packet **white choc chips**

100g packet **milk choc chips**

2 **eggs**, beaten

1 1/2/450ml mugs **milk**

3/4/225ml mug **vegetable oil**

15 large **muffin cases**

Chocolate sauce
100g **milk chocolate**

25g **butter**, measure using packet

1 mug/300ml **double cream**

2 tablespoons **soft brown sugar**

1 mug/300ml lightly whipped **double cream**

2 x 250g punnets **strawberries**

1 Preheat the oven to 180°C fan oven/200°C/ gas 6. Put about 15 large muffin cases in cake tins.

2 To make the muffins, put all the dry ingredients in a large bowl. Mix together the wet ingredients in a large jug. Pour into the bowl and mix together. Put 2 dessertspoons of the mixture in each cake case. Place in the oven for 25 minutes, or until the cakes bounce back a little when they are lightly pressed. Leave to cool.

3 To make the chocolate sauce, place all the sauce ingredients in a small saucepan and gently bring to the boil. Simmer for 30 seconds and then leave to cool a little.

4 Beat the cream until it just begins to thicken, but not really stiff.

5 Cut the strawberries into small pieces. Cut the muffin into 3 slices.

6 Assemble everything - see photo - words escape me as to how I explain this one!

Mars Bar Chocolate Sauce with Ice Cream & Blueberries

This sauce is naughty, but nice. As long as we don't eat it everyday, just for a treat, I think we will survive!

Sauce

3 **Mars bars**, chopped

1 mug/300ml **double cream**

100g **marshmallows**

tub of **ice cream**

150g **blueberries**

1 extra **Mars bar** to decorate!

1 Put the sauce ingredients in a saucepan and heat gently until everything melts.

2 Serve with the ice cream and blueberries.

Baileys Tiramisu

This wicked dessert is a great excuse to buy a bottle of Baileys. I am sure it will not go to waste and that you will make this more than once!

Chocolate sauce

25g **butter**, measure using packet

100g **milk chocolate**

1/4 mug/45g **soft brown sugar**

1/2 mug/150ml **double cream**

1 tablespoon **cocoa**

250g **mascarpone**

1 mug/300ml **double cream**

285g **Madeira cake**

2 teaspoons **instant coffee** in 1 tablespoon **hot water**

1/2 mug/150ml **Baileys**

3 tablespoons **toasted almonds**

cocoa to sift on top

1 To make the chocolate sauce, melt the butter and chocolate in a small saucepan, add the sugar, cream and cocoa. Heat gently until everything is combined and the sugar dissolved. Set to one side to cool slightly.

2 Gently mix together the mascarpone and the mug of double cream. Set to one side.

3 Cut the Madeira cake into thin strips and line the bottom of a trifle bowl. Mix the water and instant coffee together and then add to the Baileys. Pour evenly over the cake.

4 Pour the chocolate sauce over the cake.

5 Gently spoon the mascarpone mix over and gently smooth over.

6 Sprinkle the almonds on top and then sieve the cocoa over.

7 Leave in the fridge for about 1 hour. It is best eaten within 2 hours, but is also still yummy the next day.

Get out all the ingredients before you start; it makes cooking a lot calmer.

index